PRAISE FOR *THE BOOK OF COMFORTS*

"*The Book of Comforts* gives us a safe place to bring our raw heartbreak so we can align it with the refuge found in God's Word. Every page wipes a tear, holds a hand, and gives a real embrace to anyone searching for relief in the midst of their deep sorrow, suffering, or grief."

LYSA TERKEURST, *New York Times* bestselling author
and president of Proverbs 31 Ministries

"The place of grief can be one of the loneliest and most isolating places of all, yet none of us is exempt from it. This beautiful book invites us in to real stories of hardship and pain, yet also shows us that the comfort of God is more than an idea; it can be tangible in each of our lives. I feel as though this book is a perfect picture of 2 Corinthians 1:3–5, displaying 'the Father of compassion and God of all comfort, who comforts us in all our troubles so that we can comfort those in any trouble.' And I believe that's exactly what this book will do—it will be a gift to many heavy hearts and weary minds."

NATALIE GRANT, singer/songwriter

"In our damaged and disconnected world where things like loneliness, confusion, anxiety, and hopelessness seem on the rise even (and especially) in the most 'comfortable' surroundings, *The Book of Comforts* is a gift for all who are weary. It is filled with comforting images, Scripture, and thoughtful reflection, and the authors have done a masterful job not only telling us about the One Scripture calls 'the God of all comfort,' but also by showing us what His comforts look like, and where we can find them. I pray this book will help you find your rest in Jesus. It has certainly done this for me."

SCOTT SAULS, senior pastor of Christ Presbyterian Church,
Nashville, Tennessee, and author of *Befriend* and *Irresistible Faith*.

"This book is full of beauty and truth from God's Word that are sure to be a balm for any hurting heart. So grateful for the authentic voices and stories here that give space for both grief and hope. A wonderful gift to anyone you know who is walking through a season of suffering."

ELLIE HOLCOMB, Dove Award–winning singer/songwriter

"The very existence of this book bears witness that the Gospel is true. With the turn of each page you will find evidence of God's comfort in the stories and in His Scripture. What a kind and generous gift *The Book of Comforts* is to an aching world."

RAECHEL MYERS, CEO of She Reads Truth

"When I'm sitting deep in my sorrow, human words seem to bounce right off my heart. Tucked inside this beautiful book are words of a different sort—truths from the God who knows grief because He experienced it too. Where our words fall flat, God's Word gives hope."

AMANDA BIBLE WILLIAMS, co-founder and chief content officer of She Reads Truth and He Reads Truth

"As a pastor, I often search for just the right book to help point the hurting or grieving toward the beauty, goodness, and truth of Gospel comfort. During the past year, a time of deep loss for my own family, I've needed such a book for myself. I am so grateful that I've found it. You're holding it in your hands. I urge you to buy it, to read it, and to pass it on (2 Corinthians 1:3–4). This is indeed a delightful book of comforts."

GEORGE GRANT, author and pastor of Parish Presbyterian Church

"No one has a simple story, and everyone does something with their pain. This book is a beautiful, helpful guide for walking through our pain with hope anchored in God's Word. Spend time with these words and images, and I believe you will find comfort."

RUSS RAMSEY, author of *Struck: One Christian's Reflections on Encountering Death,* and pastor of Christ Presbyterian Church, Cool Springs.

"I've walked through seasons of loss and longed for a book like this—one that's full of comfort and compassion, hope and encouragement, beauty and gentle strength. This is more than just a collection of pages; it's a place any hurting heart can go to as a refuge in life's hardest moments. I plan to return to it again and again."

HOLLEY GERTH, bestselling author of *What Your Heart Needs for the Hard Days*

THE Book OF Comforts

Genuine Encouragement for Hard Times

FAIRES, FAIRES, WERNET, WILDER

ZONDERVAN®
.com

To Kendall, for bringing us together.

The Book of Comforts

Copyright © 2019 by Caleb Faires, Rebecca Faires, Kaitlin Wernet, Cymone Wilder

Requests for information should be addressed to:
3900 Sparks Dr. SE, Grand Rapids, Michigan 49546

ISBN 978-0-310-45206-5

Cover design and script: Cymone Wilder
Interior illustration: Word art by Cymone Wilder and Caleb Faires
Interior design: Lori Lynch

Printed in China

21 22 23 24 25 26 / DSC / 14 13 12 11 10 9 8 7 6 5 4 3 2

CONTENTS

Earth has no sorrow that Heaven cannot heal.

THOMAS MOORE, 1816

FOREWORD

It's hard to believe that, as I write this, my daughter Audrey would be ten and a half years old. I'm not sure what to make of that; it feels far away and close at the same time. Halfway through my pregnancy, what was supposed to be a standard ultrasound became the hardest appointment of my life.

"She will not survive after she is born."

"She is incompatible with life."

There were a host of other words, I'm sure. I remember them in bits and pieces. More than anything that was spoken out loud, what I will never forget is the way I stared at the fake flowers on the table in front of me. They matched perfectly. Too perfectly. I remember thinking that. It's strange how your mind works when you're being confronted with thoughts that are too big to comprehend in the moment.

For months I carried her, and we waited. We asked for a miracle, but it isn't what He had for us. We got to keep her for two and a half hours in this life, but I know we'll add on to that painfully small amount one day. It would be a lie if I said I don't still have moments of anger and confusion, and it would be an exaggeration to say that I've found complete peace.

I guess I'm comforted by the fact that many people I meet say the same. It doesn't make me a woman who doesn't love and trust God; it makes me a human being who can feel the ache of this life.

So what do we do with all of this? I'll tell you what we don't do: we don't burrow it away and allow ourselves to move farther and farther from God in our grief. In the midst of the pain, we have the opportunity to push back on the lies and press into the truth. He is good. I say that often, even if I don't fully understand why my version of good looks so different than His sometimes.

This is grief.

The longing for peace—if even for a moment. The feeling of comfort—if even for a night. We want to be reminded that it won't last forever, but how?

The answer, of course (you saw this coming, didn't you?), is the Word of God. I confess that I often fail to give the words the honor they deserve. I admit that I tend to go elsewhere when I've been hurt or disappointed. Maybe you do as well?

After we lost Audrey, people wanted to help so badly. They brought casseroles and told us they were praying and offered to watch our kids so we could be alone to process our emotions. They gave advice (that was not always helpful) and held us when we cried.

What I heard, over and over again, was that they didn't know exactly what to do to help. The honest answer? Make it right again. Make things the way they were before.

And the truth is that they were asking because they knew that they were helpless when it comes to the kind of help we longed for most. They felt paralyzed by the lack of ability to comfort, affirm, and empathize.

There aren't many offerings that genuinely feel like comfort. Of course there are books about loss and grief. There are practical, bullet-pointed lists designed to help you work through your sadness. But in all honesty, they weren't the things that were the most helpful to me.

If someone had handed me a book like this, I would have smiled and said thank you. I would have been grateful that I had something beautiful and full of truth and a reminder of the communal aspect of grief. Kaitlin, Rebecca, Caleb, and Cymone have done a spectacular job of putting together a beautiful, heartfelt book that invites the reader into a place where every emotion is accepted.

I hope that as you read, you remember that while all of our stories differ in circumstance, they don't differ in the common goal: to find comfort in the God of the universe through the love letter He wrote for all of us. Turn the pages and ask to find Him there. Hold this book in your hands as a reminder that you aren't alone.

Your sisters and brothers are standing with you, fighting for you, cheering you on to a place where your soul feels like it settles a little.

I pray you find that here.

Angie Smith, nationally recognized Bible teacher and
bestselling author of *Seamless: Understanding the Bible as
One Complete Story*, *Chasing God*, and *What Women Fear*

Dear Reader,

This book began the same way we hope it will end: as a conversation around the dinner table.

The four of us who worked on this book, and passed a basket of warm bread around a wooden outdoor table that day, don't have a lot in common. And yet, although our families, careers, and life stages are very different, our unlikely friendship began at the intersection of four individually and collectively painful seasons—griefs that we'd been carrying quietly. From a sudden loss to the surprises that came along with adoption to the ache of packing up and starting over, we didn't understand what one another was going through, and we definitely didn't know the words to say.

And then we found them. They were God's words. We based this book on the big idea in David's Sixty-Third Psalm: our comfort comes from God alone. But that sentence, taken by itself is hard to hang your hat on. *How* does comfort come from God? What does that comfort look like? And is He really the only true source of comfort? What about baths, chocolate, and ice cream?

The Book of Comforts was written not only out of the frustration and isolation that comes with the various aches and pains of being human, but also the simple collective refrain we can't hear often enough: *He is our true comforter.*

It was important to us that, from beginning to end, this book was a step away from grief books tied neatly in a bow or the dismal black and grays found in advice on suffering. We wrote these essays as honestly as we could, wrestling with the tension between temporal grief and the everlasting promise of comfort.

We hope that our vulnerability encourages you to join in and sit with others in their grief, to share your own stories. We're certainly in this together. We're not in this alone.

In the midst of our own terrible messes, we have come to know intimately the comfort of God. The redemptive arc of the gospel doesn't shy away from dealing with real suffering and sorrow. Christ came to bear our griefs and carry our sorrows. He is not scared by your deepest pain. He is our greatest friend and comforter. We hope this is a book you'll feel comfortable putting in the hands of your friends and family members when you don't understand the pain they are experiencing, and you don't know what to say.

Use this book as a daily guide, or open it anytime you need an extra reminder of God's hand of redemption. May we find the words of comfort in these pages together.

Caleb, Rebecca, Kaitlin, and Cymone
Summertime 2018

Comfort in God Alone

You, God, are my God,
earnestly I seek you;
I thirst for you,
my whole being longs for you,
in a dry and parched land
where there is no water.

PSALM 63:1

There is no genuine consolation but in God alone. For every need, He is the supply. For every wound, He is the cure. For every failing, He is the remedy. Is your well dry? Run to the Fountain of Life (Psalm 36:9). Is your way unsure? Listen for the sound of your Shepherd's voice (John 10:14–16). He promises to those who knock, the door will be opened; to those who seek, He will be found (Matthew 7:7). God alone is our comfort, and He supplies our every need.

CALEB

1

*"And even the very hairs of your
head are all numbered."*

MATTHEW 10:30

I hope that heaven is just one joyful realization like this after another: even our hairs are numbered by our Father. The concept of numbering the hairs on our heads may be common knowledge to us, but I wonder how Jesus' followers felt the very first time they found out. They must've been shocked that something as seemingly meaningless and mundane as hair was an intricately designed reminder of our Creator's care and compassion placed on top of our heads.

I can't wait for the "So *that's* how that works!" and "Oh, *I see* why You did that!" moments in eternity, but what I'm most looking forward to is finding the same refrain in every answer: He loves us, He loves us, He loves us.

KAITLIN

2

The LORD will be at your side and will keep
your foot from being snared.

PROVERBS 3:26

I'm always trying to steer my own feet toward safety. Manhole without a cover? No problem—veer left. Sharp cliffs over there? I'll hug the wall, thank you. It's a little harder to keep my feet safe in the tangled mess of relationships and temptations that I encounter daily. And when it comes to words and thoughts, that's where I'm in real danger.

But the way of the Lord is the way of safety. He promises to remain at our side and keep our feet from falling into snares if we follow the way of wisdom. Abiding in Him is the safest place for our bodies and our minds.

Even when dangers threaten all around, the securest place is where God has called us to be. Our own strength is not enough to block us and our loved ones from all dangers, and we cannot navigate around every obstacle no matter how careful we are. But we are all safe in the care of our Father.

REBECCA

The Lord will be at your side

3

"This third I will put into the fire;
I will refine them like silver
and test them like gold.
They will call on my name
and I will answer them;
I will say, 'They are my people,'
and they will say, 'The LORD is our God.'"

ZECHARIAH 13:9

We vastly underestimate the worth God places on our lives. If the amount He paid for us were always in the forefront of our minds, no longer would we hesitate to trust Him in the refining process. He puts us through fiery trials, not because we are disposable to Him, but quite the opposite. He considers us the finest silver and the purest gold: His children, His people.

May we rest in the truth that our lives are far more valuable to our Creator than they are to us. He will not put us through any pain without the end goal of making us more like Christ. It is a grace to share in only part of His suffering and to partake in all of His glory.

KAITLIN

4

Instead of your shame
you will receive a double portion,
and instead of disgrace
you will rejoice in your inheritance.
And so you will inherit a double portion in your land,
and everlasting joy will be yours.

ISAIAH 61:7

Imagine all the things you are ashamed of as a heavy bag of messy, embarrassing sin. You've been dragging it around for years, stuffing things inside here and there, and now it feels as if all your darkest secrets are never going to leave you. Do you imagine showing up at heaven's gates with your grimy bag of shame? Do you fear that angels will open it up and sift through it, or that the almighty Judge will upend it and make you relive each and every sin?

Take heart! That's not what the Bible tells us at all. For the children of God, all that disgrace is already paid for by Christ's sacrifice. Imagine opening a bag, expecting to find your deepest horrors, and instead discovering that it's empty. Our God is full of mercy for His children. He promises us a double portion of blessing instead of shame, and celebration in the place of disgrace.

Only in Him can our burdens be miraculously lifted. What a blessed relief that our heavy luggage of sin and shame doesn't need to be inspected every time we come and go. Bless our merciful Judge for the lifting of shame and the gift of forgiveness.

REBECCA

The Lord your God has been with you

5

The LORD your God has blessed you in all the work of your hands. He has watched over your journey through this vast wilderness. These forty years the LORD your God has been with you, and you have not lacked anything.

DEUTERONOMY 2:7

We decided to adopt because we knew we were amazing and hilarious parents. We had a delightful one-year-old daughter, and she was the prettiest, pinkest exception to every pediatrician's warnings we'd ever heard. She slept through the night right away; she ate vegetables and talked in full sentences; even her first word was *book*. She was surely a genius, and we were certainly the parents who had wrought this miracle.

Adoption was a simple, one-to-one equation to me. Children needed families; we were a family who had already demonstrably produced a wonderful child, so we were perfectly poised to welcome more children. And yet, two years, reams of paperwork, and thousands of dollars later, we found ourselves standing stupidly in the middle of a dusty orphanage in Africa as nannies thrust two screaming and terrified baby boys into our arms. I hadn't even thought to bring baby food.

During the thirty-six hours of travel home from the orphanage, I started feeling sicker and sicker and assumed I had contracted malaria. But I wasn't sick. I was pregnant. Suddenly we jumped from one baby to four in the span of about eight months. It turns out we were woefully unprepared to parent adopted children, and to do it while pregnant brought us to our knees. We weren't poised at all—we were flailing.

The years that followed inducted us into a world of pain, shame, confusion, and isolation. We are not amazing and hilarious parents. We just thought we were fantastic because we hadn't yet been tested in the dark trenches of unsolvable parenting mysteries and the muck of seeing the life we imagined for ourselves dissolve in one disappointment after another.

Don't get me wrong: we are grateful for our children. Every single one. I got pregnant with our fifth four years later, and we love all five of them. We firmly see them as blessings. God blessed the work of our hands, even though our hands felt useless at the time.

We walked through a dark period of about eight years when we felt completely hopeless about adoptive parenting and totally alone when it came to learning how to properly care for our boys. We were in the wilderness. We drifted away from each other and both retreated into depression. It felt as if we would never get help or find hope to climb out of this pit filled with traumatized children and diapers. We feared our lives were ruined, their lives were ruined, and we worried everyone would see our failure.

As the hours and the years went on, our children fell in love with one another—and that connection between them helped forge a connection for us. Even in the places where we feel the severest loss, we haven't lost everything. Loss looks different for everyone. For us, it was the loss of the life we had always imagined in exchange for one that was filled with sadness and exhaustion.

Israel, too, had its long years of sadness and exhaustion as it spent decades in the desert. Yet Moses assured the people that even when they were in the wilderness, God had been with them the entire time, and they had not lacked anything.

There's a Hebrew word, רָסַח, that is often translated as the whole phrase "you have not lacked." In other places in the Bible, it's translated as *want*, *fail*, *decreased*, *have need*, *made lower*, and even *bereave*. While the children of Israel were wandering in a season of punishment in the wilderness, Moses reminded them that they had everything they needed all along. They were not decreased. They were not made lower. They did not lack.

Even in our darkest wilderness, there is hope. God preserves us even when it looks as though all hope is lost. All things work for the good of those who love Him (Romans 8:28). Even the darkest times are for our good, and even on the bleakest days, the Lord is with His children.

It took almost eight years for us to start seeing a glimmer of hope for a rhythm of normalcy in our family. But God was there with us during those dark years. And He preserved our souls. He saved our marriage and our children. We almost foundered during those years, but when I weigh our time by God's economy, the Lord was with us the entire time. Even though we feared the darkness would never lift, and even though we thought we had nothing left, God was with us, and we didn't lack a thing.

God provides for His people. Even in the wilderness.

REBECCA

Possible

6

Jesus looked at them and said, "With man this is impossible, but with God all things are possible."

MATTHEW 19:26

There was a very long season of my life when promises about God's power and reminders of Jesus' miracles were the opposite of comforting to me. Not because I didn't believe them, but because I *had* been counting on them as my barrier to pain. But the more I learned about them, the more I took a look at my own life and didn't see the steady lineup of perfect circumstances that I'd expected. While the pages of Scripture, and my family and friends, praised God for healing and resurrection, it felt as if I were stuck on the other side of the glass, watching and hurting. There are so many days that I'm inclined to believe I know better than He does how His promises should be kept. I was furious that a promise-keeping God would allow me to slip through the cracks and experience mighty losses.

Feeling as though God let me down isn't something I'm eager to proclaim in Sunday school class, but it's hard to know His kindness and authority while also feeling He didn't use the power to fix things the way I thought was best.

No matter which side of the glass, God's story of redemption still includes you. With Him, all things are possible, and that includes healing every hurt and filling every longing, mending every unresolved place of brokenness, and nursing every confusing bout of pain. With Him, all things are possible, but redemption is sure. Thanks be to Him.

KAITLIN

7

*He heals the brokenhearted
and binds up their wounds.*

PSALM 147:3

I never would have guessed how important yellow socks would become to me. It's not a complicated story, really. Just a silly thing that reminds me of one of my favorite people. In fact, I don't think I even knew it was possible to prefer a certain color to wear on your feet, but once I learned it, you bet I teased him relentlessly and would never forget it. I certainly loved someone who had an intense yellow sock collection, and now, after his death, I miss him too.

I'll be the first to tell you that yellow socks are hard to find. They're not hanging in stores in packs of twelve or readily available in the checkout line, so finding a pair after a multi-stop search is the best feeling of all. Finding them became my own personal challenge. Although my friends and family knew the facts of my tragic loss, no one knew about the silly little details that came along with it, or so I thought.

I think the phrase "They'll find you as soon as you stop looking" applies more to grief than to dating. Now the yellow socks seem to seek me out, when the last thing I want to do is remember them. Sadness has a way of finding my hiding places, even when that spot is somewhere I thought I could count on to shield me from it, like faith.

But one day, soon after my loss, I received a brown package in the mail and prepared to add it to my existing stack of condolence cards and empty casserole dishes. Instead, it was my very own pair of yellow socks with an attached note: "Wear these when you need them most." As I put them on, standing in my own sorrow, the very thing that brought me pain was also bringing me comfort. In my deepest grief, the only consolation is someone who truly understands the depth of my hurt.

This is the kind of comfort we find in God's Word: "He heals the brokenhearted and binds up their wounds" (Psalm 147:3). He stands with us in our sorrow.

God hasn't just given us comfort for our deepest aches; He has defeated them.

He won't just provide us with kind words and wait for us on the other side of healing; He will walk with us through the uncomfortable.

God is the only One who knows how important our joys-turned-pain are to us, and He is the only One who can turn brokenness into comfort. As we read His Word, may we open our hearts to the comfort of yellow socks, and the One who knows just when to send them.

KAITLIN

8

Lord, to whom shall we go? You have the words of eternal life.

JOHN 6:68

Where do you go for comfort?

We've recently discovered a junkyard, just half an hour from our house. In the last month, I've visited it three times. Acres of rolling hills are lined with car after car, dilapidated, crushed, and disassembled. The vehicles are arranged in rows on the hillsides—in undulating waves of scrap metal. I am fascinated by the way human ingenuity can take a pile of parts and turn it into a moving, functioning automobile. But a walk through the salvage yard is also a bit like a walk through the history of broken lives and shattered dreams. Discarded old family vehicles, sleek sports cars flattened to the steering wheel, rusting frames axle-deep in the mud: the best that can be hoped for is a few spare parts.

We are inclined to insulate ourselves against real difficulty. When things go wrong, we gather what we can of the remains and try to create something functional. We live in a fallen world, and we often find ourselves in our own kind of junkyard, looking for pieces that will go back together. In a world without Christ, that's about the best anyone can do. "It's hard, but it'll get easier with time," I heard a man say. He had lost his son that year. It is hard. And it will probably get easier with time. But, thankfully, we have so much more to fix our hope on.

God is not working a grand cosmic scrapyard, making the most of broken things. He is the God of life, and He has the words of eternal life. He is restoring broken things, making them wholly new. He is undoing the curse of sin. Already He has sounded the cry of victory over death itself. Now He marches on, one heart, one soul at a time, pressing back the fall. He is the Victor who has overcome the world. The gates of hell will not prevail.

It can be hard to see His victory when we are in the trenches. Sometimes God seems entirely absent. Some seasons we seem to be only wandering in the wilderness. We toss about for answers, for help to calm our fears. We pull together whatever scraps we can find, from the world and within ourselves, or we seek distractions, shutting out whatever is unbearable. Yet none of this truly comforts. The world deceives. Our bodies are unable. Distraction only delays and compounds the difficulties. The law cannot save. Feeling will not stay. Sin destroys.

If we look to any help but Christ, we are looking in vain. Do not try to drink from empty cisterns. Do not feed on bread that does not satisfy. Christ alone comforts. He alone has the words of life. Where else shall we go?

CALEB

9

"My Presence will go with you, and I will give you rest."

EXODUS 33:14

Can you almost hear the panic rising in Moses' voice when he implored God, "If your Presence does not go with us, do not send us up from here" (Exodus 33:15)? God's presence, although sometimes a hard thing for us to put our finger on, was the distinguishing feature of the Israelites, an otherwise grouchy and reluctant group of people. Without it, Moses wondered, "What else will distinguish me and your people from all the other people on the face of the earth?" (v. 16).

Moses was actually asking a great question, and he already knew the answer. God's presence is the very thing that sets God's people apart from all other people. You can't touch it, but to Moses it was so tangible he trembled at the thought of losing it. God graciously brings His presence to His people and at the same time shields us from the overwhelming brightness of His glory. His presence means rest to His people.

Just like the Israelites, we are an ordinary people. But God has laid His hand on us and brings rest that the world cannot give.

REBECCA

THE LORD WILL ANSWER HERE AM I

ISA 58:9

10

You will call, and the LORD will answer;
you will cry for help, and he will say: Here am I.

ISAIAH 58:9

It may seem more alarming than comforting, but it's true: God answers those who seek Him, not those who are pretending to seek Him. I remember sitting on the back porch late one evening, after the kids were in bed, and praying for God's answer. *Why didn't He seem to hear? Why was I still struggling through the daily heartache over our son's insistent rejection of the gospel?* No matter how often or how fervently I appealed, there seemed to be no real answer.

Day in and day out, I had carried around with me a real burden for my son, and I thought that in my grief, I had run to God. But that night, as I prayed, I realized what I was really asking for. I was seeking freedom from trouble. I wasn't seeking God.

But God answers those who seek Him. That night I had to discard my false sackcloth and ashes. There are still heartaches enough and deep wounds that need healing. I don't have an answer to all my questions, but I have the only answer I truly need. I cried to the Lord, and He answered, "Here am I."

He has heard my cry for help. He is the God who sees. He is the God who hears. He is the God who answers with His own presence.

CALEB

11

Whoever fears the LORD has a secure fortress,
and for their children it will be a refuge.

PROVERBS 14:26

In the middle of a flight attendant's preflight safety-procedures speech, there's always a line that sticks out to me—"Parents of small children, in the event of an emergency, secure your own oxygen mask before helping those around you."

I'm not yet a parent, but I am all too familiar with the sharp pangs of responsibility that show up when you love someone fiercely. But in God's Word, peace is not found in taking care of yourself, settling those around you, or worrying about what-ifs. Security for ourselves and those we love is found in fearing the Lord, who has given us a safe refuge. He has already secured us as His children; may we rejoice in our Father's protection.

KAITLIN

12

"I will not leave you as orphans; I will come to you."

JOHN 14:18

The Rialto Bridge in Venice carries thousands of feet across the canal each day, but I was on the lookout for six specific feet. Belonging to my mom, dad, and brother, these feet had left America the day before and boarded a plane to visit me in Italy, where I was studying for a college semester. A few months without my family felt like a lifetime, especially when we were separated by oceans and I could not text my mom about my sudden allergy to Italian laundry detergent.

So, although I'd planned to show off all of my grown-up European knowledge, I was thrilled that the day to hug my parents' necks and to remember the scent of my brother's cologne had finally come. We'd set a time and a place to meet—the top of the Rialto Bridge—and I'd taken the early train to meet them and make sure I wouldn't miss a thing. But as soon as I stepped out of the train station, I was enveloped in crowds of people, confused by the twists and turns of cobblestone, and I suddenly forgot the Italian words for "right" and "left." I was lost. Ultimately, I found the bridge and the reunion I'd been looking forward to, but not without several detours along the way.

Sometimes the concepts of family and community seem so far away, even when we're trying our best to find them. There are gaps of hurt and voids of grief in my groups of closest people, those that will not be whole again until we cross the bridge to eternity. Some of us are orphans who have never met our blood relatives, while others are orphans who have never felt known by them. But that is the very setting of the conversation that was taking place with Jesus and His disciples in John 14. As they huddled around a table, with broken bread, He revealed that His chair would soon be empty, introducing the grief His family of followers didn't know was coming. With reminders that His physical body would be gone, and yet He would still be with them, Jesus also told them to eat bread and drink wine in remembrance of Him.

As we look around at the roughness of our families or our lost sense of belonging, I wonder if we, too, can take communion with the broken pieces, holding both a sense of longing and a taste for what's to come. If we allow brokenness—including our families—always to be a reminder of the wholeness of Christ, we will never despair. Our place in the lineage of Christ, paid for with His own blood, secures our spot as children of a loving Father.

God puts the lonely in families (Psalm 68:6). While our eternal birthright is sure and promises to fulfill all voids and longings, our earthly relationships may not be what we expect. Still, their fractures point us to the deep fullness of Christ's love. When we embrace the shattered pieces of our expectations, we remember Christ's body, broken for us. And when we find others doing the same, partaking of the bread and the wine with broken hearts, even though they may not be blood, they are family.

Families are more than Thanksgiving Day plans and obligatory phone calls. They are more than the hurt you face when going home or the voices you haven't heard in far too long. They are a gathering of lost-and-found orphans, waiting together in hope. God puts the lonely in unconventional families of believers to proclaim His glory.

No matter who you find yourself surrounded by today, your family is not lost. You will not be left alone. May each of your encounters be a step that carries the gospel in your heart, a bridge to our eternal abundance with Christ. And each time our families feel broken, may we savor Christ's call to remember Him, for our Father is with us.

KAITLIN

I WILL COME TO YOU

13

"I will make rivers flow on barren heights,
and springs within the valleys.
I will turn the desert into pools of water,
and the parched ground into springs."

ISAIAH 41:18

When I'm in pain, I want to rush through it and resume my life as soon as possible. But this is not how God works. In fact, some of His biggest plans for us take place during seasons of wilderness. He doesn't rush through deserts the same way He doesn't overlook our griefs, big and small—each is handled with care, and none is left alone.

After all, without the barren heights, deep valleys, dry desert, and parched ground, we would never see the flowing rivers, rich springs, and pools of water He has promised to us. We may dread seasons of drought, but dry ground is the needed foundation for God to provide. By itself, it has nothing left to offer unless someone waters it with a promise of renewal. When we are emptied of ourselves, we can finally give up the pretense of self-reliance and confess we have nothing left. The driest seasons in our hearts make for the holiest ground in our lives. May we look expectantly for the Lord and His hands of provision. He will withhold no good thing.

KAITLIN

14

*"All those the Father gives me will come to me, and
whoever comes to me I will never drive away."*

JOHN 6:37

God's grace, His undeserved favor, is the surest and most profound comfort for the believer. It is comforting because it is not dependent upon how good we've been or how deserving, intelligent, winsome, or confident we are.

We come to Christ because God gives us to Him. It is not because of something we've done. It is because God is good and full of grace. God is love and entrusts us in love to the care of His Son, Jesus Christ. What greater security can there be than the everlasting and unconditional love of God the Father?

And we are entrusted into the most caring of hands. Christ Jesus has suffered and has been tempted yet is without sin. On the cross He bore our griefs and carried our sorrows, so He is able to sympathize with our every weakness.

Rest in the grace of God's fatherly love. Cast yourself into the caring hands of Christ, for He will not turn you away.

CALEB

15

Surely he took up our pain
and bore our suffering,
yet we considered him punished by God,
stricken by him, and afflicted.

ISAIAH 53:4

My family lives on the side of a small hill surrounded by walnut trees. But I dream of the mountains. So, at great expense and trouble, my husband and I try to find and show a few snow-covered mountains to our children. It's not easy to schlepp them across the country while making accommodations for five different appetites, opinions, and music preferences on the road. But once, when we'd arrived at the appointed place, we turned to them and celebrated. "Look! What beauty! Have you ever seen such magnificence?"

But my most honest child shielded his eyes from the cloudless sky and turned his face downward, sighing. "It's too bright. I can't look out there. How soon are we going to eat?" And this is honestly how I feel sometimes about God's sacrifice for me. It's just too great to understand. It's too bright for my mind to comprehend. Instead of looking into the face of this unfathomable mystery of love, I'm inclined to go find some supper.

But I believe—just like my kids seeing the mountains—the mystery and weight of Christ's sacrifice sticks with us. Even if I'm unable to catch it the first time, even if I can't take it all in at once, I keep coming back for more. He took my pain and bore my suffering. What beauty! What incomprehensible magnificence!

REBECCA

HE TOOK
UP OUR
PAIN

16

"Everyone who calls on the name of the LORD will be saved."

JOEL 2:32

There are a lot of terrible things that can happen to us. In today's scripture, the prophet Joel is warning Israel about a plague of judgmental locusts on their way to decimate all the grapes, oranges, and grain in their path. Sometimes it helps me to compare a problem to a plague of locusts. Is this better or worse than a swarm of ravaging bugs? The comparison helps me keep the small stuff in perspective. God is with His children even in small things.

But some problems are actually worse than biblical plagues. Jokes about insects fall to the wayside as a colossal wave of grief washes everything else away. Yet, even then, God is with His children just the same. No matter what looms over us, everyone who calls on the name of the Lord will be saved. The broken and the scared are invited to call on His name.

He is the only answer to our fears. He is the only solution to our griefs. This is the gospel. His sacrifice brings our peace. Everyone who calls on the name of the Lord will be saved. Call on His name.

REBECCA

EVERYONE WHO CALLS
ON THE NAME OF THE LORD
WILL BE SAVED.

Comfort in Praise

I have seen you in the sanctuary
and beheld your power and your glory.
Because your love is better than life,
my lips will glorify you.
I will praise you as long as I live,
and in your name I will lift up my hands.
I will be fully satisfied as with the richest of foods;
with singing lips my mouth will praise you.

PSALM 63:2–5

God's abiding presence is our greatest comfort. And more than comfort, His presence inspires us to bear the fruit of overflowing praise. He grants to us joy in the wastelands, full satisfaction in the barren places, and the peace of His great love. There is great comfort to be found in looking upward to Him, rather than fixing our eyes on temporal pains and sorrows.

CALEB

17

The LORD your God is with you,
the Mighty Warrior who saves.
He will take great delight in you;
in his love he will no longer rebuke you,
but will rejoice over you with singing.

ZEPHANIAH 3:17

I never would have guessed that Batman knew how to do the hokey pokey. And yet, at my little brother's fourth birthday party, he proved me wrong. Ever since he demonstrated to a group of toddlers how to "put your right foot in and shake it all about," I haven't been able to look at Batman the same way. But at least now I know what happens in the Batcave on a slow night.

My brother's fourth birthday party was a day we'd looked forward to since our mother took us to the store to buy matching Batman and Batgirl capes and masks weeks earlier, promising an appearance by "the real Batman" very soon.

Our favorite place to wear the costumes was the grocery store. The first time we accompanied our mother on an otherwise-routine trip wearing our capes and masks, we'd discovered fate in the form of a kiddie ride. Standing just inside the automatic sliding doors and basking in an air-conditioned breeze, the ride would hold both of us, it only cost a quarter, and a familiar theme song confirmed our every hope: it was the Batmobile. We didn't have to do all of the bringing. The joy had followed us, and it was with us.

Suddenly all of our public cape-donning appearances were validated and encouraged. The store manager noticed our costumes during the grocery runs that became more and more frequent, and he'd seek us out to distribute stickers and applause. The delight was no longer just ours! We brought it to others, and they shared in it with us.

But one day we'd tied the capes' strings around our necks and secured our masks, approaching the grocery store and its squeaky sliding doors as usual. Only this time we'd removed our masks in disbelief, finding the Batmobile replaced with a happy, clapping neon dragon that said, "I love you" on repeat.

We didn't feel loved. In fact, it was quite the opposite. Our mother encouraged us to take our feelings to the store manager, who seemed to be hiding from a miniature sobbing Batman and Batgirl.

If I'm being honest, sometimes I feel the same way when I approach God. When I first began to read His Word, I was hesitant, only to continue and discover that the heart I'd been carrying around all these years longed to match His. It belongs. I'd trusted Him more, singing songs about His goodness and expecting each encounter to be more wonderful than the next, and it was—until it wasn't.

One day I showed up to God with scripture and prayer, only to find my circumstances falling apart and my heart continuing to break. In Romans 8:28, Paul said, "In all things God works for the good of those who love him," but I couldn't see how one ounce of it could be good.

This pain was the tipping point. I could no longer imagine how a God who was with me and knew my fears would still allow this to happen. It didn't feel like love. It didn't feel like the love of someone I knew well. Had God been wearing a costume all along?

And yet, even when we're unsure of what He is doing, God is

rejoicing over us. It's hard to believe that—just like worship—suffering is a vehicle for seeing more of God's glory. Pain is the arc of the gospel story, the one thing that we all hope to avoid but that Jesus walked into willingly. Our days may be filled with deep disappointment, but the God we've praised during the greatest joy remains with us. He delights in us. And even if we hurt too much to remember His goodness today, He will never stop rejoicing over us with singing.

KAITLIN

LET YOUR *Hands* BE STRONG

18

"Just as you, Judah and Israel, have been a curse among the nations, so I will save you, and you will be a blessing. Do not be afraid, but let your hands be strong."

ZECHARIAH 8:13

It is not lost on me that before reading today's scripture, I went to a physical therapist—to strengthen my hands. You see, it's easy to take the command to "let your hands be strong" as a criticism, something a coach would bark at us from the sidelines: *Hustle! Don't drop the ball!*

But it's not. The nations of Judah and Israel? They must've felt as if they had been sidelined, without money to survive or peace to carry on. And I'd bet that today you may feel that way too.

It's easy to focus on the weakness of our hands and forget we were created by Someone else's.

The only way to let our hands find true strength is to allow them to rest in God's. May our feeble hands latch onto the comfort of knowing He is strong, both without us and for us.

KAITLIN

19

"Young women will dance and be glad, young men and old as well. I will turn their mourning into gladness; I will give them comfort and joy instead of sorrow."

JEREMIAH 31:13

I wonder if you have to first experience a bit of mourning and sorrow to understand true gladness and comfort. Obviously, no one is running out to find their taste of sorrow while on a Saturday-morning trip for coffee and donuts. Regardless, sorrow seems to find us, whether we suit up and get out of the house or stay quietly at home. But once we have experienced heartache, God's words of comfort sink in and resonate in a new way.

Do you wish your sorrows had never come? Me too. Every day. I wish the world weren't broken and families loved each other forever. I wish we didn't have to say goodbye to people we love. I wish my body wouldn't get so tired.

God promises to give us lasting comfort and joy instead of sorrow. But He doesn't follow our time line. So, while there may still be mourning today, He promises us the hope of joy. And our sorrow enables us to experience the richness of His comfort.

REBECCA

Joy instead of sorrow

I have drawn you with unfailing kindness

20

The LORD appeared to us in the past, saying: "I have loved you with an everlasting love; I have drawn you with unfailing kindness."

JEREMIAH 31:3

Some claim summer starts when the days become warmer, but I am a firm believer that the season cannot begin without a Jell-O poke cake.

My mother taught me how to make one when I was seven years old, using the same recipe she'd learned when she was young, surrounded by the mixing bowls and kitchen counters of her childhood home. The cake is nothing fancy, filled with artificial ingredients and authentic delight—and I think that's precisely why I love it so much. This harbinger of summer is made by poking holes into a perfectly good cake, and while it seems destructive at first, the end result is always worth it.

When I was younger, I'd sit on a stool, watching my mother make it, dipping my fingers in the whipped cream topping and licking it off when she turned her back. As I grew older, when summer blew her first warm wind, we'd look at each other and know exactly what to make for dessert.

Each year it becomes easier to remember the goodness tasted in seasons past. Poked holes are less of a catastrophe when you know they won't remain empty. It's easier to wait when you know what's coming. In the same way, God's past kindness serves as a reminder to us—as we experience our current voids and emptiness—that His love overshadows and outlasts our hollow seasons. The care He uses to fill our sad days isn't a new recipe based on our circumstances. Instead, it's like the familiar, joyful rhythm our hearts and hands find at the beginning of summer and in that first taste of a faithful favorite. We can wait because we know exactly what's coming—or, in this case, *Who* is coming.

May we recall God's character in the past, notice His constant faithfulness, and look forward to His future compassion. Thanks be to Him, whose love is everlasting and whose kindness is unfailing.

KAITLIN

21

Is anyone among you in trouble? Let them pray. Is anyone happy? Let them sing songs of praise.

JAMES 5:13

The day I met Rebecca, she invited me over to her house for egg salad and raspberries. We were coworkers, the only two squeezed into a ten-foot-by-ten-foot office like two college roommates. Within hours of meeting, she'd offered me sparkling water, introduced me to her Great Dane, and muttered a German phrase when something didn't go quite right. I was sure I liked her already. A former theater teacher, Rebecca now had a new job that involved shipping labels instead of stage directions, but she ended each day by saying, "We're doing so great," as if the workday had all been a successful dress rehearsal.

While we both loved Broadway show tunes and could play the flute, the lives we went home to after work were very different. Rebecca had four children (with another on the way) and an adoring husband, while I barely knew anyone in the city I'd just moved to on my own. Even though she already had more than enough mouths to feed, she was never hesitant to add one more to the family dinner table, where Bess the Great Dane would hunt for crumbs beneath my feet and Rebecca's children would entertain me with memorized facts about bald eagles. When the meal was over, Rebecca would send me home with leftovers and sheet music, her kids standing at the top of the driveway to wave goodbye. "You're doing so great," she'd say. And when I drove from their house back to my own little apartment, I knew I'd found home. With Rebecca, I was comfortable enough to stretch out in God's kindness and call it exactly what it was—good. And our office songs and delirious laughter had become praise.

But it wasn't always that way. In fact, Rebecca was with me the early morning I got the absolute worst news—my brother had died unexpectedly in an accident. I will never forget the way her mouth rounded the words "Lord, have mercy." Intent on getting me to my parents as soon as possible, she looked up flights, then determined she'd deliver me to my family herself. We began our hours-long road trip with silence, my black dress in the back seat. Sometimes I would sob, but mostly I was shocked, beginning a sentence only to trail off, realizing the story would be completely different from now on. "Lord, have mercy," she continued. It didn't change what had happened, but she was creating a home in a place I never wanted to go.

I used to think the world was divided into good-news people and bad-news people, those with a stroke of luck and those without. Consequently, I lived in fear of becoming a bad-news person. But when I became one, I experienced what Rebecca had been showing me all along: our immediate need for the nearness of Christ, no matter our circumstance. We need equal measures of Him in both our "You're doing so greats" and our "Lord, have mercys."

Life as God's children includes not just a possibility of happiness and trouble, but rather a guarantee of both. However, as we experience joy and hardship, worship offers us a way to continue giving and receiving the one thing that holds the two together: God's glory.

May our lives become one rhythmic refrain of His goodness, not separated by good or bad news, but unified by His care for His children in both. Today, let our lips express our prayers and praise to our Father, who has created a home for us.

KAITLIN

22

"Open wide your mouth and I will fill it."

PSALM 81:10

A small finch built her nest in the corner of a potted plant on our back porch. Soon her eggs hatched, and we saw the baby birds as they grew. We watched each time as the chicks heard the flutter of her wings and strained upward with open mouths, expectant. Each time she brought them food unceasingly, until they were filled.

An open mouth is a sign of need. Though we often think of need as negative, God calls us to hunger, to thirst, and to want. He desires for us to need, deeply and expectantly, and He delights in providing for us unceasingly.

Do you hunger and thirst? Do you ache for His provision? Open your mouth wide, and He will fill it.

CALEB

OPEN WIDE YOUR MOUTH & I WILL FILL IT

Psalm 81:10

I, EVEN I,
AM HE WHO
COMFORTS YOU

ISAIAH 51:12

23

"I, even I, am he who comforts you."

ISAIAH 66:13

Have you ever seen a mother comfort a dirty child? Children are dirty at least 50 percent of the time anyway, but it's still a little surprising to see a fresh and clean mother cradling a child with a bloodied nose or mud-caked trousers. When a child needs comfort, a mother doesn't think of maintaining her distance to keep herself clean but scoops up the child and gets right to the business of comforting.

In the same way, our Father comforts us, not at a distance, but in His arms, getting bloody and muddy. Bring your fears and hurts to the One who comforts you. He does not flinch or retreat from the burdens you bring, from the wounds that undo you. You will find peace in His loving embrace.

CALEB

24

"For you who fear my name, the sun of righteousness will rise with healing in its wings, and you will go out and playfully jump like calves from the stall."

MALACHI 4:2 CSB

Fearing the name of the Lord is the condition set for claiming the promise in today's scripture. What does it mean to fear the name of the Lord? Although the word *fear* commonly evokes an image of cowering, in this context *fearing* God means regarding Him with reverence and awe.

We are built for awe, and we long to be inspired by things that are greater than ourselves. Consider how you feel when you see the sun setting over the ocean. That feeling of awe doesn't diminish our humanity, but rather it enlarges our capacity for love and understanding.

Honor the Lord, and He promises to joyfully bring blessing and laughter. Fear His name and take Him up on His invitation to celebrate and rejoice.

REBECCA

The Sun of
righteousness
shall rise
with healing
in its wings

25

"I will make you a wall to this people,
a fortified wall of bronze;
they will fight against you
but will not overcome you."

JEREMIAH 15:20

We sold our house the same week our fifth baby was born. We had to move out before we were ready to close on our new place. That meant we spent a very vulnerable month living in spare rooms at gracious friends' houses. During this month, one of our seven-year-old sons was getting into a lot of trouble at school. This was nothing new for him, and it is part of our family lore that he was sent to the principal's office on the first day of kindergarten.

I tell myself that helping kids through tough times is much easier in your own home (also easier when you don't have a new baby), but it's always hard. And our champion was going for the gold medal in mischief. *Look at his endurance! How does he have the creative power for such astonishing misdeeds? What form and poise he has under interrogation!*

Every bad report hurt me. I felt as if everything he did were physically piercing my skin. My soft, pouchy exterior is no match for the cruelty of my own child. Because I was falling apart, I had no wall to protect him or the other children. Hunched over, nursing a newborn on a makeshift sofa, I looked at tiny infant fingers clutching at a borrowed quilt, and I felt there was nothing to support us.

But the Lord can turn a weary woman into a wall—a fortified wall of bronze. Strong enough to protect her little ones behind and strong enough to withstand attacks from outside. And somehow, heartbreakingly, strong enough to bear cruelty even from the protected space behind the walls. Through the love of our family and the patient understanding of a few friends, God brought us through that hard season. We felt powerless, but He gave us strength we never could have imagined for those days. Our God is mighty, and He promises to give us His strength to make us into walls of protection. I still field attacks from both sides of the wall, but I am safe because I know I will not be overcome.

REBECCA

I AM WITH YOU TO RESCUE YOU AND SAVE YOU

26

"I will make you a wall to this people, a fortified wall of bronze; they will fight against you but will not overcome you, for I am with you to rescue and save you," declares the Lord.

JEREMIAH 15:20

I learned to sail at the same time I taught my first sailing students. I was sixteen, working as a lifeguard at a summer camp in Michigan. Barely older than the campers, I volunteered for a rotation out on the lake, teaching a sport I'd never learned myself. Although I didn't know a jib from a mainsail, I was sure I'd pick it up. How complicated can it be to sit in a boat and let the wind blow you across the water?

On my first day out, the wind was strong, and as we were coming about, the boom swung violently across the deck, throwing me and my two hapless campers into the lake. We bobbed, helpless, as I watched the sailboat's mast slowly dip from pointing skyward to disappearing under the water, like a Fun-O-Meter when all the cheers have died down.

After the boat was humiliatingly towed back to shore by more experienced seafarers, I spent hours hammering the hard metal pins to reattach the rudder, which had been mostly torn off. The sharp, metallic sound of my labors could be heard by everyone I had hoped to impress, and all my penance never yielded a functioning sailboat again.

The totally fruitless pinging of that hammer still rings in my ears when I try to lean on my own strength. In the first half of this verse, the

Lord promises to make us into a fortified wall—strong and dependable. But in the second half of the verse, He completes the picture: our strength comes only from Him who rescues and saves us.

We have to hold these two ideas together: because He is a strong rescuer, we can be strong too. Even though my bravado tells me I'm a master sailor and a competent shipbuilder, I'm just a clanging gong apart from His strength.

REBECCA

27

"I am like a flourishing juniper;
your fruitfulness comes from me."

HOSEA 14:8

Five minutes after I stepped into the lecture hall to teach my first class, I knew I was in trouble. My students waited with quiet expectation, but I remained silent. The only sound was the soft rustling of paper as my hands searched my notes for anything—just one gem of an idea, one story, one fact, one talking point. The hours, the weeks, of preparation seemed to have vanished, and I was left silent, with nothing more to offer.

Have you ever come up short? Even with our best preparations, we don't always hit the mark. In fact, most of the time we miss it completely. Often it is because we have spent our days striving after wind. We seek hope, security, success, and wisdom in earthly storehouses instead of running to the treasures of Christ. We are prone to fix our hearts on earthly promises of satisfaction and success, only to find we have squandered our affections on empty idols that cannot save. But God heals even our waywardness. The empty wells and the dried-up orchards are reminders that our fruitfulness comes from God alone.

This is the promise He gives: He is like a flourishing tree, always green, always abundant. He favors those who turn to Him. What comfort there is in this! He does not leave us to hope in the works of our own hands, but receives us graciously, washing away all our folly, covering us with His sheltering wings. He answers and cares for us and blesses the work of our imperfect hands.

CALEB

be still
and know
that I am God

28

"Be still, and know that I am God;
I will be exalted among the nations,
I will be exalted in the earth."

PSALM 46:10

When I was a preschooler, I was the Queen of the Playground. In retrospect, the details of how I came to reign are a little fuzzy, but I am certain it was based on a thorough campaign emphasizing change and compassion for the people.

With fire-engine red Keds and curlicues for hair, I truly desired to serve and protect my fellow classmates, while occasionally expecting them to indulge my love for affection and nursery rhyme recitation at a high decibel. Every day I'd skip through the gravel, climb a ladder, and keep watch over games of tag and patty-cake from the top of the slide.

One day I looked down from my post to see my classmates screaming and running away from a large mound of dirt. I slithered down the slide and ran over, gravel flying in my path. Upon arriving, I realized it wasn't just a menacing pile of soil—it was a hill specially crafted by dozens of crawly red ants.

I did what any queen would do: I lifted my red Keds and began to stomp on our party of intruders. I did not expect, however, that they would fight back. Soon I was covered in ants and their respective bites, wailing and waiting for my mother to pick me up early. Not a good look for royalty.

When tragedy hits, it's our instinct to swirl into action—making plans, casseroles, phone calls, and home visits. Our creaturely desire is to fix things—and quickly. We long to stomp out the sting of any wrongdoing we've performed or injustice we've received. Yet God's response to our hurt goes against what we'd like to do: He asks us to be still.

But He doesn't ask us to be still and complacent, to be still and give up, to be still and wallow. Rather, we are to be still and know who He is. And when we do, may we find that trusting Him is the most productive, loving, transformative thing we can do for ourselves in our pain. Maybe He doesn't stomp out the ache the way we'd like Him to, but He laces up His own version of red Keds and stands with us, feeling the sting and serving as our comfort all at once. Let us be still before Him today, for our King will take care of us.

KAITLIN

29

*[The Lord] said to me, "My grace is sufficient for you,
for my power is made perfect in weakness." Therefore
I will boast all the more gladly about my weaknesses,
so that Christ's power may rest on me.*

2 CORINTHIANS 12:9

We had launched our canoe into the Harpeth River late that morning. The shade from the trees overhanging the banks kept us comfortable through the heat of the day. We stopped for a late lunch, pulling off onto the shallow gravel embankment—two lean guys ready for lunch. The rocks were cool beneath us as we shared sandwiches, chips, jerky, and cold drinks. My friend and I were both in that space between daunting job and life decisions. Charting the courses for our families, ministries, and callings, we both felt a little displaced.

This quiet river was swollen from recent rains and moved at a steady pace. I like deep rivers, and I enjoy the challenge of quick currents. I don't have enough experience to pilot my canoe on rougher courses, and the Harpeth was enough of a challenge that day. Life lately had been a challenge too. Somehow I'd found myself on rough waters the past few years, and my steering wasn't what it needed to be. I felt as though I'd been raked over the rocks, tipped over, and tossed in the undertow far too many times. I was burned out at work, burned out at home, and quick to lose heart.

"I'm not as strong as I thought I was," I confided to my friend, paddling quietly. "Sometimes I think weakness is all I have."

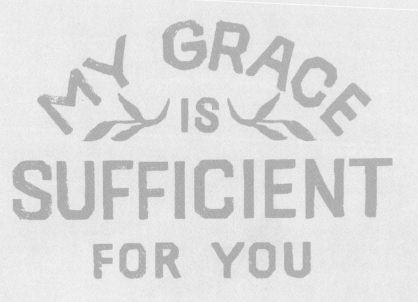

He nodded. I was glad he wasn't quick to speak. He didn't need to. He simply concurred. *Yes. We are weak.*

Whether we are facing daunting circumstances now, or they lie ahead, or we have come through a wearying storm, we often feel inadequate, even completely undone. But this is where God wants us. His purpose is to make us the kind of people who realize our need for Him. We may want to grow into self-reliant and autonomous supermen or superwomen, captaining our own ships across mighty waters. We may want *our* power to be made perfect. But it is God's power, bestowed by His grace, that is the real point. "My power is made perfect in weakness," He reminds us. And nothing opens our eyes to His grace and power like a confrontation with our own insufficiency.

We may set our bark on the waters, but we are not reliable sailors. Like the disciples, we, too, see the storm hit, and we are at a loss, crying out, "Lord, save us! We're going to drown!" (Matthew 8:25). But all along, He is there. He is there to be our strength, for He captains not only the boat but the storm and the coursing waters as well.

Do not fear your weakness; rather, yield it to Him. And may the power of Christ rest on you.

CALEB

I WILL REFRESH the WEARY & SATISFY the FAINT

30

*"I will refresh the weary
and satisfy the faint."*

JEREMIAH 31:25

Parenting four children under four years old brought the
weariest days I have ever experienced. Our adoption of two
boys was proving more difficult than we had ever dreamed, and
we felt lost and isolated, too ashamed to admit how desperately
we needed help. I remember spending endless gray hours spoon-
feeding babies, too weary to rouse my imagination to consider
the good days that had come before or to hope for the good days
that surely would come after. When it comes to babies, we say,
"Yea and amen" even when we don't see the yea or the amen.

I still carry the scars of that weary season with me. The
memories of those feelings of failure and shame haven't gone
away just because other people seem to have suffered more or
because time has passed for me. Our sorrow can continue to
hang around our hearts like cobwebs, years after the pain has
passed.

Today's scripture is a promise to all the children of God. Your
weary soul will be satisfied. You will have as much joy as you can
bear. He will restore you. Even if you feel as if you have walked in
muck for years, He promises you will have joy unthinkable. He can
even brush away the most stubborn cobwebs around our hearts.

And He promises you that your weary days will not have the final word. Sadness and exhaustion come to us all, in varying shades of ugly, but we have a promise that is unshakable: He will satisfy and refresh us. May He do it even now!

REBECCA

31

Praise the LORD, my soul;
all my inmost being, praise his holy name . . .
who redeems your life from the pit
and crowns you with love and compassion.

PSALM 103:1, 4

Maybe it's something unusual to aspire to, but I have always wanted to be a tour guide. During the spring semester of my junior year of college, I studied abroad in Florence, Italy, and as part of a cultural immersion program, we were given the opportunity to volunteer as English-speaking helpers in various historic locations. I was assigned to Santa Croce, a gorgeous Franciscan church with a flair for simplicity and art that sprawls into the lively city square that surrounds it.

Mostly I picked out baseball-capped dads and their sneaker-wearing families from their panic-stricken disorientation in the square, promising them air-conditioning, directions to their destination, and a little art history along the way. Their relief at being found by someone who spoke their language reflected the legacy of stories that took place inside Santa Croce—a lost people who'd gather to worship and pray, pronouncing the syllables of Scripture that sounded more and more like home.

Saint Francis of Assisi founded Santa Croce, choosing to build a church next to the Arno River. However, he had no way of knowing that long after his life was over, this decision would place his beloved church directly in the path of Florence's most historic flood. He wouldn't know how bad the damage would be, or if the basilica would be salvageable, or even if anyone would want to take care of it, but centuries later, telling the story of its reconstruction was my favorite part.

As I stood in the basilica, pointing at the repairs that had taken decades, I'd show how high the water was when it streamed through the church's doors, the floors that had been painstakingly repaired, and the parts of its original structure that remained. It didn't take long for those on my tour to realize what I already loved about this building: they were standing on beams of restoration. I was a tour guide through a tried-and-true redemption story.

And although I turned in my tour guide badge at the end of the semester, it's my joy to point out something I don't want you to miss either: you, too, are standing on a framework of hope. The storms and sadness have come, but here you are, held upright by God's strength. He redeemed your life from the pit before, and He will surely do it again. He is leading you through His own true redemption story. Whether the troubled waters are rising or falling, may we look to our Redeemer.

KAITLIN

32

In all this you greatly rejoice, though now for a little while
you may have had to suffer grief in all kinds of trials.

1 PETER 1:6

When I'm miserable, rejoicing is often the last thing on my mind. Peter's first letter to the saints includes a whole barrel of reasons to rejoice when we are suffering.

Consider these reasons to greatly rejoice:

1. God's mercy is great (1:3).
2. We have new birth in Him (1:3).
3. He is our living hope (1:3).
4. We have an inheritance that will never fade (1:4).
5. Our inheritance is in heaven (1:4).
6. Our suffering only lasts a little while (1:6).
7. Our suffering results in praise, glory, and honor (1:7).
8. He offers inexpressible and glorious joy (1:8).
9. We have salvation for our souls (1:9).
10. The word of the Lord endures forever (1:25).

Scripture truly tells us, even when we are miserable, we have endless big reasons to rejoice. Hold on to this hope, and God will enable you to rejoice, even in the midst of suffering.

REBECCA

He
GRANTS
PEACE
TO YOUR
BORDERS

33

He grants peace to your borders
and satisfies you with the finest of wheat.

PSALM 147:14

If you could draw a circle marking the border of your peace, how large would it be? Maybe it would span the walls of your home or wrap around your loved ones. It might cover those circumstances that feel under your control or those days that progress exactly the way you hope. When this happens, does your circle grow bigger? Does it produce more peace? What about when it doesn't happen?

If your circle of peace feels small today, you are not alone. Find comfort in this: God's borders of peace do not wax and wane with the threat of bad news. Our Father surrounds His children with a relentless, endless, loving embrace. May we walk in the peace of being called His.

KAITLIN

Comfort in Dark Places

On my bed I remember you;
I think of you through the watches of the night.
Because you are my help,
I sing in the shadow of your wings.
I cling to you;
your right hand upholds me.

PSALM 63:6–8

For those of us who rest in Christ, the darkest hours and the stillest silence are but the shadow of His wings over us. There, think on Him; sing to Him; cling to Him. He does not leave us but brings us help. He upholds the restless, the weary, and the downtrodden. Keep watch, wait, and remember Christ, your "very present help in time of trouble" (Psalm 46:1 NKJV).

CALEB

PRIVATE—KEEP OUT
TRESPASSING AND
LOITERING PROHIBITED
BY LAW
13

Your DAYS OF SORROW WILL END

34

"Your sun will never set again,
and your moon will wane no more;
the LORD will be your everlasting light,
and your days of sorrow will end."

ISAIAH 60:20

My dad says his first book will be called *Jagged Edges.* It's not something he's always declared; he began saying it when our party of four became a family of three. Ever since the September day when the first winds of fall ushered in my brother's last breath, my parents and I have become keenly aware of how relentlessly the months come and go, and how we desperately wish we could get "normal" back. Now, every missed birthday, table setting, holiday tradition, or normal Tuesday is a sharp reminder of both the good thing we used to have and the horror of no longer having it. Jagged edges.

It's in moments and lifetimes like these that we realize the comfort the world has promised us will no longer suffice. The things that used to bring us joy become sore reminders of the discomfort we cannot escape. But this isn't a surprise to Jesus. In fact, it's quite the opposite. He leverages our expectations about life on earth, warning us that we will have trouble in the world (John 16:33). Because of His love for us, jagged edges are guaranteed, but they are not eternal. He has overcome the world.

May our unmet expectations and our pain lead us to the hope and promise of their redemption. We will outlive our sorrow with the endurance of hope. Thanks be to God for edges jagged and smooth.

KAITLIN

35

"I am the light of the world. Whoever follows me will never walk in darkness, but will have the light of life."

JOHN 8:12

Every night I turn off the kitchen light and walk through the living room, feeling the familiar worn wood under my feet on my way to bed. On most nights, it's smooth sailing, but occasionally I am surprised by a literal giant black monster, with his head, huge and hairy, at the same height as mine. Darkness makes everything—even our faithful old Great Dane—more uncertain, dangerous, and scarier than it is in the light.

Spiritual darkness is even more terrifying than the dark of night. We can't see clearly to judge what is right and what is wrong. Spiritual darkness takes away our ability to see the world as it truly is. We are unable to see what is dangerous and what is safe. Without Jesus' light, everything is muddled. Some people walk their whole lives in darkness; they are so accustomed to it that they don't even know they are in it.

In the dark, I can't tell what's in my path. I misinterpret the signs and mistake family pets for monsters. There is always something to fear in darkness. But Jesus is the Light of the World. He gives us light to see what is wrong and what is right, and He teaches us not to fear but to walk in His safety.

REBECCA

I AM the Light, OF THE World

Blessed *are the* poor *in spirit*

36

"Blessed are the poor in spirit,
for theirs is the kingdom of heaven."

MATTHEW 5:3

The Beatitudes suspend a limbo stick and ask, "How low can you go?" This verse emphasizes humility and reminds us of our place in the kingdom of God. And yet, suffering doesn't just lower our spirits—it crushes them. Reminding us of our human limits yet again, it's humbling and painful. But blessed?

Being poor in spirit isn't so much about attitude as it is about living with an awareness of need. When our spirits know exactly what they lack, they will pursue it until they find it. God is who a humble and poor spirit thirsts for.

A lowly and lacking spirit is one fit for the kingdom of heaven, where all longings will be met in the fullness of our Creator. When we realize our need for redemption, we find belonging with our Redeemer. What a blessing indeed.

KAITLIN

YOU WILL BE COMFORTED

37

*"Blessed are those who mourn,
for they will be comforted."*

MATTHEW 5:4

Casserole deliveries are never a good sign. The first one arrived on a Monday, shortly behind the worst news we'll ever receive. Death had visited early that morning, taking everything we knew with it.

Baked in a throwaway aluminum container and left on the doorstep, the layers of meat and cheese carried strong scents of old comfort we could no longer inhale. It marked the beginning of our grieving, which seemed too active a verb for our repeated acts of helplessness—sitting, sobbing, wailing, waiting.

Reminders were constantly showing up at the door, but none of us would dare say the word *dead*, and even now I only use it in the context of reminding God what He allowed to happen.

Sitting huddled in the living room between flower deliveries and sympathy cards, we pieced together a fitting obituary column, sending our truth away to an editor who had the power to rearrange the sentences but not our situation.

Neighbors would pick up our bundled words from their driveways and read them at their breakfast tables. Then they would close the paper, clean off the bread crumbs, and throw it away. We would not.

The end of one life marked the beginning of a new one for the rest of us, marked by black dresses and grief that seemed to maintain rather than burst. Anniversaries, holidays, and old voicemails would treat us as if we were supposed to move on and collect our joy again. We did not.

Although we try our best, we can never fully comfort one another. Yet even our most imperfect efforts are not wasted, for they point us to the ultimate satisfaction and eternal joy that await us.

At the time, comfort seemed impossible, and it's true that we will not be fully whole and comforted in this life. But as Christians living between the "already" of Christ's sacrifice and the "not yet" of His return, we find our suffering is infused with a rare hope that speaks volumes of comfort.

We rejoice knowing that Christ doesn't just hold our hands until the happy ending—He mourns with us. Our grief is His grief, and our pain brings Him sorrow. He understands our pain, and He does not leave us alone in it.

Comfort would not find us in the form of casseroles or condolences, in the activities we used to enjoy or the songs we used to sing. Although it would look different than expected, comfort wouldn't be any less promised to us. Now we only have an appetite for true comfort—eternal joy, kept promises, and true words. God's Word reminds us that we, as mourners, are not forgotten. The circumstances we never would have chosen for ourselves have been called by name by God, who covers them in the truest form of comfort: His blessing. It is enough.

KAITLIN

38

"Do not worry about tomorrow, for tomorrow will worry about itself. Each day has enough trouble of its own."

MATTHEW 6:34

I love to see babies being born. When I get to work as a doula, I love to cheer for laboring women. And there's a simple secret to the whole ordeal. You just have to find a way to keep the panic under control. In the moment, everything is impossibly hard; it's been hard for hours, and it will be harder still for a few hours more. That fear is really big and overwhelming, but you have to relax into that fear one piece at a time. Each contraction has to be its own little wave to handle—one at a time. And breathe.

Life can feel like one long birthing process. If we think of all the pain we've already been through and anticipate all the possible hard things to come, it's more than we can bear. But we aren't alone, and even in those seasons when every consolation seems absent, we have the promise of God's continuing love. Even when we feel alone, we are assured of God's purpose and provision. His goodness is the beginning, middle, and end of our stories.

REBECCA

DON'T BE
Afraid;
JUST
BELIEVE

39

*Jesus said to Jairus, "Don't be afraid; just
believe, and she will be healed."*

LUKE 8:50

I am prone to lose hope. As a father of five children, I desire to see
them all well adjusted and hungry for Christ. What happens when
one of them wanders? The waywardness of a son is a deep grief. My
wife and I have sought to love him, bring the gospel to him, and find
resources to aid him in his struggles, but we have been met with deceit,
distrust, and dangerous behavior. At night, he has risen from bed and
vandalized the house, endangering us all. I am prone to fear. After
seven years of heart-wrenching struggle, I cry out, "How long, O Lord?"
I am prone to lose hope.

Do you believe that Christ can mend? Jairus's daughter was dead,
yet Jesus said, "She will be healed." Not even the dead are beyond the
reach of our Great Physician. No loss, no grief, no tragedy is beyond
the power of Christ to restore, to console, to mend. Do your fears
steal away your sleep? Think on Him in the watches of the night. Does
your heart ache with unbearable loss? This, too, will be healed. Jesus
hears our griefs and knows them well, and He gives His sure words of
comfort: "Don't be afraid."

CALEB

Nothing will harm you

40

"I have given you authority to trample on snakes and scorpions and to overcome all the power of the enemy; nothing will harm you. However, do not rejoice that the spirits submit to you, but rejoice that your names are written in heaven."

LUKE 10:19–20

We had been eyeing him for about an hour, and he had been eyeing us. Wild goats have a strangely intelligent look about them, and this one, standing on the outcropping above us with his shaggy white beard and deep-brown eyes, seemed especially enlightened. On a family men's retreat on the lake, with all the in-laws and cousins watching, we were happy for a little extra excitement, and the goat was just the thing. Along the banks of the Cumberland Lake, there are rock cliffs, a series of loose geologic layers that provide a good wall for scaling. So, up my cousin Tim went, after the goat. He never made it to the top. About halfway up he stopped, pulled his left hand away from the crevice he'd been gripping, and leapt into the water. He had been stung by a scorpion. By the time we sent Tim on the boat toward the docks and the emergency room, his arm had ballooned up to twice its size and had begun to turn purple.

I'd like to be able to trample on snakes and scorpions without a care. We'd all like our challenges solved, those stings that can be so crippling in our daily walks. But we often lose sight of eternity. When our eyes are downward, on the snakes and scorpions, we miss the real point of Christ's promise to His disciples.

Christ offered these two consolations:

In this life, we need not fear the power of the enemy. Christ's promise to the seventy-two disciples who were gathered around Him was a reminder that He supplies all we need for the calling He has given us. This doesn't mean we won't face challenges and even heartache. It means He will go before us. His grace is always sufficient. His provision is always fitting.

We have cause for greater joy: Our names are written in heaven. We are His. That is our true comfort. He has written our names in His book, and we are eternally secure. When the enemy comes, seeking someone to devour, and even when we feel his sting, we can rest on Christ's unfailing promise and the inheritance He has fully secured for us.

CALEB

41

"See, I lay a stone in Zion, a tested stone,
a precious cornerstone for a sure foundation;
the one who relies on it
will never be stricken with panic."

ISAIAH 28:16

Riding in the midnight wilderness of darkest Peru, I feared for my very life, and although I'm prone to enjoy the dramatic, I was longing for the safety of home. Six months earlier, when my college friend Joanna invited me to join her on a visit to her husband's family in Lima, I figured it would just be two weeks of casual Andean fun.

And it was. I experimentally spoke Spanish, we shopped for green oranges at the market, and we rode in the back of pickup trucks. Her in-laws were welcoming, and we ate guinea pigs, played soccer, and bought alpaca hats. We decided to top it all off with a much-anticipated trip to Machu Picchu, one of the wonders of the ancient world and a great place for a fascinating hike.

Here's what you need to know: Joanna and I went to Machu Picchu alone. It was a long way from Cuzco, so we stayed in a hotel at the base of the mountain before we climbed. And after a full day of breathtaking explorations, we were ready to find a ride back to Lima.

We didn't want to spend too much money, so instead of finding a charter bus or a taxi, we listened to a local guy who latched onto us as we walked to the base camp. He promised to drive us back home and assured us he wouldn't take any other passengers. It didn't seem great, but it was inexpensive, and Joanna thought it would be okay.

A red flag should have gone up when we got to his tiny car and found a man already waiting there, ready to join us on our ride. I barely understood Spanish, but as the hours passed, Joanna started murmuring to me that strange things were happening. Our driver was making plans over the phone and reporting that his passengers seemed calm. He alerted the person on the other end of the line where and when he would arrive. When we neared Cuzco, he drove away from the route home and into a shady part of town. Joanna nudged me and whispered that we should run if we got the chance.

Suddenly the car pulled over and each of four men, in perfectly synchronized movement, started coming to each door of the car. Before they could get there, Joanna locked her car door while I flung mine open and ran away down an alley. Joanna managed to extricate herself with more dignity and found me panting with my hands on my knees. We flagged down another taxi and huddled together in the back seat all the way home.

I still don't know what exactly happened that night in Peru, but I was afraid for my life. Have you ever feared for your life? The terror of the unknown and the fear of imminent harm can shake us to the core. Panic sets in, and we are thrown into utter confusion. Scary things happen all the time.

In this world we may encounter dangers, toils, and snares, but we rest on an unchanging, unshakable foundation. We may tremble, but the ground beneath our feet is secure. In Christ we will not be confounded.

But how can this comfort us when we are afraid? How do we apply the concept of "a peace that surpasses all understanding" (a paraphrase of Philippians 4:7) right here and now? There is a difference between being stricken with panic for physical safety and stricken with panic in the soul. In today's scripture, God promises not that we won't encounter frightening things, but that deep down inside, we have an eternal security that is not shaken by circumstances, even terrifying ones.

Even in the face of terrible, real danger, our souls are in a place of security. Sometimes victories don't make any earthly sense, but we are more than conquerors in Christ, and even the scariest rides can't touch that eternal security.

REBECCA

42

From six calamities he will rescue you;
in seven no harm will touch you.

JOB 5:19

It seems straight out of a board game instruction manual, doesn't it? Narrowly escape six calamities to gain a path to freedom after the seventh. Fall down six chutes but climb up one ladder. Go to jail six times, followed by passing go and collecting $200.

Sometimes I believe I must certainly be getting closer to hitting my "suffering quota," at which point all of my circumstances will suddenly march uphill, improving with greater speed and bigger success into eternity. Yet this isn't what we are promised. Pain is not a result of rolling the dice or an angry gamemaster—there is much more at play than what we can see. We can't see our opponent who roams about, seeking to devour us and our joy. But we also can't see the God who has already taken care of him, claiming you as His child and His joy to be yours.

Through Christ's resurrection and defeat of our enemy, the game has been won. We are safe, and harm doesn't stand a chance against God, who fights for us. May our minds draw away from the calamity and closer to our Rescuer.

KAITLIN

HE
WILL
RESCUE
YOU

43

As a father has compassion on his children,
so the LORD has compassion on those who fear him.

PSALM 103:13

When my first baby was still a baby, I used to dream about a magical day with no crying. Babies don't care what you want or how your ears feel, and crying is their most powerful weapon. When I hear someone else's newborn crying, I can usually manage to stay calm, but the sound of my own baby crying is biologically programmed to make me feel desperate—or at least alert—and keen to do anything to help that tiny person stop crying. I like all babies just fine, but I am crazy for my own little ones.

God's ear is attuned to our cries. We're not just another cute baby in the nursery to Him. We are His beloved ones. And when He hears our cries, He promises to bring us to a safe place. Babies do grow up, and I saw that cry-free day after about three years of waiting for it. But we will continue to bring our heartbreaks to our Father every day of our lives. It's okay if we never have a cry-free day. And unlike new parents, our heavenly Father will not get desperate or panicked by our constant requests. He is long-suffering, patient, and infinitely wise to comfort His children.

REBECCA

44

*"If you belonged to the world, it would love you as its own.
As it is, you do not belong to the world, but I have chosen
you out of the world. That is why the world hates you."*

JOHN 15:19

I grew up in Asia on the mission field and attended an international school, surrounded by kids from all over the world. We were a mishmash of cultures and all got along pretty well, though I mostly kept to my own classmates and friends. When I was in third grade, I rarely mingled with the fourth-graders because they seemed so much older and I was intimidated, but there was one boy who seemed to look at me the wrong way each time we were on the playground.

I don't even remember why we got into a fight, but I remember the look in his eye, and I remember the thought in my heart. He hated my guts. He was taller than I was, but skinnier, and I was just stupid enough to think I could take him. The fight didn't get very far. I think we slapped at each other, but we both felt tough and justified in our enmity. By the time the teachers stepped between us, my analog Mickey Mouse watch—the first watch my parents bought me—was in pieces on the ground.

Hatred takes many forms, from outright rage to smiling disdain, but in each case a line is drawn. Just as in an old western, someone is saying, "There's not room enough in this town for the two of us." When pride straps on its six-shooter, it becomes hatred. While we cross paths with hatred in some form almost every day, and even carry it about in our own hearts, when we face hatred head-on, bristling for a fight, it can be shocking.

I don't like to be hated, and the thought that someone out there harbors contempt and malice toward me is unsettling. What did I do to deserve anyone's hatred? Yet when we find the eyes of the world looking at us in the wrong way, we have great reason to be encouraged. Christ offers this good word: *The world hates you because you do not belong.* These are surprising as words of comfort, but they are nevertheless reassuring. When I am on the receiving end of hatred because of my faith, I immediately want to ask, "Why? What did I do?" Jesus' answer is here: "I have chosen you out of the world."

If you find yourself swimming upstream, buffeted by constant opposition as you yield yourself to the work of the kingdom, be of good courage. The world does not love you. Our aim is not friendship with the world, but deep and abiding friendship with God. He chose us and has given us a new life and security that cannot be shaken by the most powerful hatred.

In a world full of sin, conflict is unfortunately normal. It is an enmity that has been normal since the serpent spoke in the garden. The spirit of the world is full of malice, envy, spite, and self-seeking, but the Spirit of Christ declares, "Love one another" (John 15:17 NKJV). And this mark of love in the life of God's children is ours because God first loved us and chose us out of this world so that we might be His own possession (1 John 4:19).

CALEB

I
HAVE
CHOSEN
YOU

45

Indeed, he who watches over Israel
will neither slumber nor sleep.

PSALM 121:4

Sometimes I sleepwalk. It's not something I plan the evening before when I lay out my clothes for the next day, but I have been known to go on mini home expeditions without waking up. Occasionally I'll find souvenirs in my bed from that night's adventure—anything from kitchen spatulas to bathroom soap—with no recollection of leaving my bedroom.

When I was growing up, my father struggled with insomnia. In my childhood home, my parents' bedroom faced mine, a staircase dividing them. More than once, I'd jolt awake in the middle of the night to find my dad's arms on my shoulders, preventing me from sleepwalking (well, falling) down the stairs. While sleeplessness isn't something I would wish on anyone, my dad's restless state truly kept me safe.

God keeps the same kind of watchful, protective eye over us, but it is of no deficit to Him. He doesn't lose sleep because of our troubles or lack energy after helping us. It is His joy to watch over you. Trust Him to do so today.

KAITLIN

HE WHO WATCHES
OVER ISRAEL
WILL NEITHER
SLUMBER
NOR SLEEP

46

Cast all your anxiety on him because he cares for you.

1 PETER 5:7

I first came to Tennessee because my life was over anyway, and this seemed as good a place as any. I hadn't gotten into my number one college pick, and it didn't seem as if the sun was ever going to shine again. As I rode south with friends to check out another college, my expectations were already very low. But I was really caught off guard when our first meeting with the college administrators was held in a living room.

This is how I first met the Wilburs. Their living room was painted yellow and filled with books and movies I'd never heard of. They put cinnamon in their afternoon coffee and seemed interested in what I had to say. Little did I know how much these people would shape my life.

I don't call classical music "classical" because Greg Wilbur's voice in my head reminds me that classical is a time period, not a style. I call it "art" music, no matter how pretentious I sound. My taste in books and movies was influenced by the Wilburs' shelves. I fell in love with my husband over notes we passed in Greg's classes. Sophia Wilbur knew I was pregnant with my first baby before I even thought to take a test. We have walked together through quiet heartbreak. They gave my husband his first oil portrait commission. The Wilburs have believed in us and loved us for our whole adult lives.

But sitting in their humble yellow living room, petting Molly, their long-haired, short-legged dog, I couldn't have known that lifelong friends were serving us the first in a long line of mugs of cinnamon coffee. I just knew that this college wasn't what I was planning, and these people weren't what I had expected.

God cares about our little anxieties. At the time, my college prospects seemed like the only thing that mattered. But God brought such goodness and acceptance to my life because of that first rejection letter. And as the rejections continued into my adulthood, His unchanging love was the steadying force. He gives us the good gifts of His Word and His people to comfort our hearts. We need comfort for the big things—like unbearable infertility—and the small ones—like a flooded kitchen.

Dear friends are a testament of how much God cares for us. All comfort comes from Him, but sometimes His comfort looks like coffee cups, buffalo pizza, and weathered canary walls. We can cast our cares and our anxiety on Him, and He will bring us comfort in joyful, unexpected ways.

REBECCA

47

"I will give you a new heart and put a new spirit in you; I will remove from you your heart of stone and give you a heart of flesh."

EZEKIEL 36:26

When it comes to certain areas of my life, I feel as if my heart is made of stone. Sometimes I can't forgive or let things go. I want to change—I want to be able to think about things differently—but I just can't see my way straight. My heart feels set in its ways. I want to be free and be a new person. I want to be able to forgive and move on with my life. I want to stop taking things so personally. But I can't change my own heart. I can't break free of the sickening, concrete-hardening bent of my heart.

Have you ever felt like this? I get in deep ruts, and I know they are the wrong ruts. But it's so hard to climb back out. I speak in the same patterns; I feel my feet returning to the same habitual places.

And I can't break free. I don't have the right sledgehammer to unjam my hardened ways. As soon as I realize this, I'm already headed one step in the right direction. I can't fix this myself. Haven't we all tried?

The Lord makes us new. He gives us a new heart, a new desire, a new song. He gives us new passions and new inclinations. But He is the One who does it. He removes that heart of stone; He doesn't just change it a little—He makes it new.

He is making all things new. Even our tough old hearts.

REBECCA

I WILL
GIVE YOU
A NEW
Heart
AND PUT
A NEW
Spirit
IN YOU.

48

"So do not fear, for I am with you;
do not be dismayed, for I am your God.
I will strengthen you and help you;
I will uphold you with my righteous right hand."

ISAIAH 41:10

I am frankly shocked by how frequently the words "do not fear" appear in Scripture. Fear is a habit for many of us. But Jesus, the angels, and the apostles remind us again and again that our instinct for fear is hindering us rather than helping us. These reasons not to fear are from Isaiah 41:

1. God is with you (v. 10).
2. He is the first (v. 4).
3. He is the last (v. 4).
4. He called you from the farthest corners of the earth (v. 9).
5. God has chosen you (v. 9).
6. He promises to strengthen you (v. 10).
7. He will uphold you (v. 10).
8. He tells you not to fear (vv. 10, 13, 14).
9. He will answer you (v. 17).
10. He promises you will rejoice in the Lord (v. 16).

When fear creeps into the corners of your mind, remember these promises. When you are safe in the Lord, what can you fear?

REBECCA

I WILL STRENGTHEN YOU AND HELP YOU

49

*"Do not let your hearts be troubled. You
believe in God; believe also in me."*

JOHN 14:1

How many problems have you tried to solve by letting your heart be troubled? When something is wrong, we let it furrow our brows and lower our heads; we drag our feet or raise our voices. When our hearts are troubled, it shows in our bodies.

Christ reminds us that our belief in God has a direct bearing on whether or not we allow ourselves to be downtrodden. If we believe in God, and we believe that He gave His Son to redeem us, it suddenly sets things back in perspective. Lift up your head, and let not your heart be troubled: Christ has come to set things aright, and He came to give you hope.

REBECCA

do not let your hearts be troubled

YOU WILL BE SATISFIED

50

"Blessed are you who hunger now,
for you will be satisfied.
Blessed are you who weep now,
for you will laugh."

LUKE 6:21

Many of my favorite memories include flour dust, rolling pins, and recipe testing in my mother's kitchen. For us, baking always kept pace with the seasons, from gingerbread houses to blackberry pies and brownies just because; the cabinets always seemed to be standing by with each and every required ingredient. But one day aches and pains crept in, warning us of a season we'd no longer want to savor. Tucking away the cookie cutters and leaving the mixer under the sink, my mother peered into the cabinet, asking, "Will I ever use sprinkles again?"

It was a silly question, but one we truly didn't know the answer to. But at such intersections of doubt, fear, and uncertainty, we find the promises of God and the truth that's never failed us. Blessed are we who are included in the full circle of Christ's redemption—from hunger to satisfaction, from weeping to laughing, from sinner to beloved. In other words, yes, we will use sprinkles again. Thanks be to Him.

KAITLIN

BE Strong AND COURAGEOUS

51

*Be strong and courageous. Do not
be afraid or discouraged.*

1 CHRONICLES 22:13

There was a time in my life when strep throat was the worst-case scenario. I was a seven-year-old girl who adored school and hated doctors, especially doctors who wanted to ram oversized Q-tips down my throat.

My younger brother held the same opinion about strep, but for him it was the antibiotics. I'm not sure who thought it was a good idea to flavor the already-terrible children's medicine with sweetened hot-pink syrups, but my brother, who didn't like desserts anyway, wasn't fooled. So when sickness season came around and a nurse tried to soften the diagnosis with promises of "pink bubblegum!" and "strawberry milkshake!" we cried in unison.

One winter night the situation was especially bleak. We had the misfortune of not one, but two cases of strep throat. My brother resisted the prescribed medicine like a champ, pulling out just the right number of tears and kicks to send our family's dinnertime peace into an immediate nosedive.

"You'll love the pink bubblegum!" my parents pleaded.

"Your favorite—strawberry milkshake!" they tried, knowing it was false.

He needed backup. Enter yours truly, his seven-year-old sister, to the rescue. I jumped into the middle of the spat, motioning for him to climb on my back. Piggybacked and void of socks, jackets, or plans, I opened the door and whispered, "We're running away. I won't let them get you." We ran out the back door and into the woods, only to abandon our plans and return home after hearing the first noise we couldn't identify.

I hated my little brother's pain and wanted to help him find comfort as soon as possible. But finding temporary comfort wasn't the same thing as healing.

God doesn't like our pain either, but His plan for us is better than our just escaping it. He wants to heal us and redeem us, providing each of His children with an active hope and eternal comfort. But we can't always see the ways He's doing this, and many times we may wonder if we're still on His agenda at all. This is why we need strength and courage too—to bridge the gap between hurt and healed.

God tells us to be strong and courageous because He knows we will want to listen to the pain rather than to His promises. He knows we will want to find our own solutions and escape routes, and He understands we will struggle to trust His plan is good when it feels anything but. Our fear is not a surprise to Him, which means He has anticipated it and prepared for it with the gift of His Word. Because of these promises, we can be brave.

KAITLIN

52

He strengthens the bars of your gates and
blesses your people within you.

PSALM 147:13

There are only so many things we can do. We can buy the sturdiest lock, the safest car, the strongest medicine, the biggest lifeboat, the healthiest meal, and the stickiest bandage. We can follow the directions, clear the pathway, send a warning, look both ways, and call for help. We can do all of these things tenfold, and bad things will still happen to us. We can prepare for the worst, and it can still be more horrible than we ever imagined.

Even our best attempts at self-preservation depend on the Lord. And while our attempts may fail, His will not. It brings God joy when we discover His deep well of strength and choose to rest in it. We are in good hands, and there we will remain.

KAITLIN

Comfort in Restoration

Those who want to kill me will be destroyed;
they will go down to the depths of the earth.
They will be given over to the sword
and become food for jackals.

PSALM 63:9–10

We face real opposition, both physical and spiritual. When the enemy comes, seeking our destruction, we are promised the rich comfort of God's justice. He sees all the workings of men, and He opposes the proud and the unjust. More than this, He does not leave injustice unanswered but sets the world right. He makes all things new.

CALEB

THERE IS SURELY A FUTURE HOPE FOR YOU

53

There is surely a future hope for you,
and your hope will not be cut off.

PROVERBS 23:18

Hope is an all-or-nothing: either you have it, or you don't. It can't be found in the seams of your empty pockets or made by the craftsmanship of your two hands. It doesn't depend on a sunny attitude or a warm day, an upturn in luck or a decision made. Hope was born before you, breathes without you, and beams within you. It is not a pleasant thought to get through the moment or a distraction from a present hardship, but a trusty bridge from here to eternity.

Hope is an all-or-nothing, and because of Christ in you and for you—today, right now, and forever—it is an all.

KAITLIN

54

People of Zion, who live in Jerusalem, you will weep
no more. How gracious he will be when you cry for
help! As soon as he hears, he will answer you.

ISAIAH 30:19

Do you put off calling on the Lord for help? It's tempting to look first to the solutions of man. We try to solve problems with money or advice. If we're short on money, we try to make more. If we don't know what to do, we look to the crowd for a solution. But what if problems and solutions don't come in equal batches? What if there is an ever-present source of help for us in times of trouble?

Go to the source. Don't begin on the fringes. When we hesitate to call out to the Lord for help, we put off the one thing that can actually bring healing and justice. He offers us an end to weeping and a gracious ear when we call for help.

Run to your watchful Father, for as soon as He hears, He will answer you. Bring your darkest fears and your deepest secrets; bring your heartbreak and your embarrassment. There is One who is attentive to your heart.

REBECCA

I WILL
RESTORE YOU

55

*"I will restore you to health
and heal your wounds,"
declares the LORD,
"because you are called an outcast,
Zion for whom no one cares."*

JEREMIAH 30:17

No matter how hard I try to carefully gather each piece of laundry from the dryer, something is always left behind. Days later, I'll find an abandoned sock on the stairs or still waiting to be picked up from the washing machine. I always feel a little bit apologetic for the senseless mistake I've made as I pick it back up.

No one wanted anything to do with Zion, leaving them feeling just as abandoned as the lone sock. The entire city and ground where the temple stood was considered a waste, no longer worth tending to or caring for. No one wants anything to do with sickness or injury either. It's never something we would choose for ourselves. And yet, just as the Lord was near to Zion, He is near to us. Promising to restore their health and heal their wounds would have been enough, but He does more than that. He instills purpose in their pain. *Because* they are outcasts, they are able to know the One who cares when no one else does. The places we are quick to abandon and label as lost causes, God restores. Just as He knew the ins and outs of the city and its demise, He knows the coordinates of your pain and will faithfully pick you up and remain by your side.

KAITLIN

A STRONG FOUNDATION

56

A thousand may fall at your side,
ten thousand at your right hand,
but [harm] will not come near you.

PSALM 91:7

In his hymn "The Solid Rock," Edward Mote reflected on the glorious security we have in Christ. He wrote, "Though all around my soul gives way, He then is all my hope and stay." This image of unchanging security in the midst of upheaval is a welcome comfort.

When everything around us seems to be collapsing, we are prone to be anxious about the things to come and downtrodden about the things that have been. When everything in our lives seems to be falling apart, when entanglements, disease, terror, and destruction surround us on every side, we fall to fear and despair. Yet even then, God promises, He is our refuge. He is our sure foundation and our shelter amid the storm.

Does the battle rage around you? Have all your trusts and securities vanished? Run to Christ. He will be with you in trouble. In the shadow of His wings, you may rest secure because He has promised, "I will rescue; . . . I will satisfy. [I will] show My salvation" (from Psalm 91:14, 16).

CALEB

I WILL

Heal

you

57

"'This is what the LORD, the God of your father David, says: I have heard your prayer and seen your tears; I will heal you. On the third day from now you will go up to the temple of the LORD.'"

2 KINGS 20:5

The things that often seem evil to us—sickness, trouble, toils, snares, dangers, oppositions, griefs, losses—these also are God's ministers. He uses all things for good to those who love Him (Romans 8:28). In the midst of such difficulties, we are quick to forget this. We are quick to forget that God is good all the time, even when the times are evil.

The healing God offered Hezekiah was already planned from the beginning. God's covenant with David was that his house would be the root of an eternal kingdom, yet at this time Hezekiah had no son. God did not forget His covenant, but provoked Hezekiah that he might see God's goodness and faithfulness in all things. Hezekiah would see that God could call him back even from the brink of death. He is a faithful God, and no matter what, He keeps His covenant.

This same God has made a covenant with us, a covenant of salvation, sealed by the blood of Christ Jesus. He is the faithful One, who does not forget His own but brings justice and salvation to His people.

Take comfort: God hears the prayers of His people (1 John 5:14–15). He knows our griefs and sorrows (Psalm 56:8). God heals and binds up our wounds (Psalm 147:3). He is already working (John 5:17). He has prepared the way, that we may enter His sanctuary (Matthew 25:34).

CALEB

58

They will have no fear of bad news;
their hearts are steadfast, trusting in the LORD.

PSALM 112:7

We all instinctively know what the worst news would be—the news that makes us shudder when we think about it. When something goes wrong, we first reassure each other that it's not the worst news: "Mom, we're all okay, but we've had a fender bender." So, when the psalmist asserts that we will have no fear of bad news, it's a steep promise to fulfill.

I've been sitting with these words for a week now. And the longer I think about them, the more I love them. I want to have no fear of bad news. I realize that bad news will come. I've seen it blindside those I love. But somehow God's people don't have to live in fear of it.

Notice the psalmist didn't say, "Bad news won't hurt." When bad things happen, it hurts. But thinking about the future doesn't have to hurt. God gives us steadfast hearts, and we don't have to live in fear. When the bad news comes, the Lord will be there with us, and we will walk that road together.

When we trust in the Lord—trust Him with our days and our nights, our jobs and our houses, our kids and our siblings—we need have no fear of bad news. He holds our future in His omnipotent, omniscient hands. He knows what will come, and we can't change the future by fearing it.

Rest in His provision for your future. Let your heart be steadfast, trusting in the Lord, and have no fear of bad news.

REBECCA

THEY WILL HAVE NO FEAR OF BAD NEWS

59

*"They will fight against you but will not overcome you, for I
am with you and will rescue you," declares the LORD.*

JEREMIAH 1:19

When I took up kayaking, it seemed like the perfect sport for
calculated adventure. Although waves rushed beneath me, I was
in control, armed with a paddle and a sense of direction. No matter
how high or fast the water came toward me, I could steer away from it,
zigzagging between the currents. As a beginner, I learned to navigate
the river in a group with an instructor. Like a football coach during a
time-out, he'd call for us to huddle around him in our kayaks before
each waterfall drop. After teaching us the exact strokes and angles
we needed to know to make it through to the next huddle, he'd then
lead the way, showing us how to effortlessly glide over the rocks and
through the water. It also helped to know that if something went wrong
and we drifted too far or got stuck on a rock, he would be there to
help us.

But during one of our group huddles, instead of presenting a game
plan, he only issued a warning: "At the bottom of this waterfall, you're
going to fall out."

Sometimes I feel as if God tells me the same thing. I used to think
He wouldn't give me more than I could handle, until He did.

"You're going to fall out, mess up, lose control, and find fear."

Suddenly we don't care what it takes to paddle upstream against the current. We'll do anything to avoid falling out. Anything to avoid our worst-case scenario.

And yet, I wonder if we've gotten this worst-case scenario thing all wrong. Maybe we've been too scared about what it means to truly consider it. Have we ever dared to look past it? Through the fall and pain and fear? So you fall out. The worst possible thing happens. Then what?

My only choice was to paddle down the waterfall and hope for the best. Just before the bottom, I hit a rock and soon found myself upside down in the water. Yet I'd been so afraid of this moment that I'd never thought about what to do next. I hopped back in my kayak and continued paddling down the river to join the rest of the group.

Christ has already faced our true worst-case scenario: separation from the only One who can truly comfort us. This doesn't mean we will no longer face pain, but we will face it, and it will not destroy us. We will fall out, mess up, lose control, find fear, and it will not overcome us. If we look past the pain, we will see God's rescue, again and again. And that's something to rejoice over.

KAITLIN

60

"Listen, King Jehoshaphat and all who live in Judah and Jerusalem! This is what the LORD says to you: 'Do not be afraid or discouraged because of this vast army. For the battle is not yours, but God's.'"

2 CHRONICLES 20:15

Jehoshaphat became the king of Judah when he was thirty-five. A vast army was headed his way, and Judah just didn't have the resources to fight them off. Jehoshaphat declared to God before his people, "If calamity comes upon us, whether the sword of judgment, or plague or famine, we will stand in your presence before this temple that bears your Name and will cry out to you in our distress, and you will hear us and save us" (2 Chronicles 20:9). He was ready to accept anything, but their first line of defense was a cry to the Lord for help.

He asked God to judge the incoming pagan army, declaring his obedience and dependence on God: "We do not know what to do, but our eyes are on you" (v. 12). Notice that he wasn't looking at the danger marching toward him; his eyes looked to the Lord.

God spoke through a man in the assembly, and He gave these incredible words: "Do not be afraid or discouraged because of this vast army. For the battle is not yours, but God's. . . . You will not have to fight this battle. Take up your positions; stand firm and see the deliverance the LORD will give you, Judah and Jerusalem. Do not be afraid; do not be discouraged. Go out to face them tomorrow, and the LORD will be with you" (vv. 15, 17).

They took God at His word and headed to their positions praising

God and singing, "Give thanks to the LORD, for his love endures forever." In the meantime, God caused the advancing armies to turn on each other, and the enemies of Judah destroyed one another. With His praises still on their lips, God's people came to the place that overlooked the appointed location for the battle, only to find a field of dead bodies. No one had escaped (vv. 21, 23–24).

The Lord did the work. His people had nothing to fear. They responded to His reassurances and victory with praise. This passage is a primer for trusting in God. When we are confronted with terrible danger, first we must cry out to our God. Then we listen to His words. The Bible is our ready source for the true and relevant words of God. Finally, we praise Him. The earth is His, and all that is in it is made to praise Him. We can't control outcomes anyway, but we can look to the One who does.

REBECCA

THE BATTLE IS NOT YOURS BUT GOD'S

61

"In that day," declares the LORD Almighty,
"I will break the yoke off their necks
and will tear off their bonds;
no longer will foreigners enslave them."

JEREMIAH 30:8

Freedom. It's a word that puts fresh, salty air in our lungs and sunshine on our faces. We all want to be free. The image of broken bonds cues the "Hallelujah" Chorus in our ears. But humans are funny. God made us for worship, and we are built to praise and serve Him. But when we are left to our own devices, we will just move from one slavery to the next.

Have you ever found yourself free from one idol only to find you've replaced it with another? In *How Should We Then Live*, Francis Schaeffer said, "People are unique in the inner life of the mind—what they are in their thought-world determines how they act." Humans will find something to worship, and we let it shape our whole world.

The freedom the Lord promised in Jeremiah isn't just the freedom of social justice; it's not simply the freedom to live, work, or speak as we wish. He's giving us freedom from all of it. He's giving us freedom from the idolatry of the world. He's liberating us from worldliness.

Our King brings justice greater than we can imagine. And He brings us freedom beyond our biggest hopes.

REBECCA

62

The Lord is faithful, and he will strengthen you
and protect you from the evil one.

2 THESSALONIANS 3:3

I never wanted to join the club of sufferers. But once I became a member, the first thing I wanted to do was look to those who had gone before me. Although I'd never wish on anyone the pain it takes to join the club, when it became my turn, it was suddenly comforting to know others had faced similar pain and still remained standing. I wanted a guide—a mentor—to tell me all of her best, most helpful encouragement that would plant my own feet in truth.

But today I do not take it lightly that you are opening this book in hopes of dog-earing the same type of comfort. And while I don't have much to offer that you probably haven't heard before, I do want to print in bold italics the single piece of consolation that sustains me and is so easy to forget: ***God has never made an empty promise. He is faithful.***

His commitment to us is full and unwavering. It is filled with faithfulness for us, His beloved, and healing for the brokenness from our past days that still haunts us. It is filled with strength for us, His people, to sustain us today, no matter what hurt or delight today may bring. It is filled with protection for us, His children, covering with compassion all of the unknowns we have yet to imagine. The Lord our God can be trusted to watch over us forever, His promises remaining unbroken. May we respond with the fullness of our trust. Hallelujah, hallelujah.

KAITLIN

YOU SURROUND THEM WITH YOUR FAVOR AS WITH A SHIELD

63

Surely, LORD, you bless the righteous;
you surround them with your favor as with a shield.

PSALM 5:12

One summer my mother learned to make quilts. Sitting in the living room of a friend's home, she'd follow the instructions to cut squares of fabric, join them together to mimic a pattern, and carefully sew for hours, watching her envisioned design take shape.

When I graduated from college, her gift to me was, of course, a quilt. But not just any quilt! It was the compilation of fabrics we'd chosen together several months earlier. It was all of my favorite colors and prints—mustard yellow, deep purple, and swirly florals. I moved to a new city and began a new job, but every night I slept under the covering of the design my mother had imagined from the beginning. When I held it up to my face, I could smell the joy of perusing the aisles with my mother and choosing just the right bolt of fabric. The scent of her choosing me.

My brother was next on her list to receive a quilt, but we didn't know he'd make it to heaven first. My mom put away her sewing machine and allowed the grieving to begin. But a few years later, while visiting my parents, I noticed she had taken it out of the box. Next to it was a pile of familiar-looking fabrics, and as I thumbed through them, I recognized them immediately: they were from my brother's old dress shirts. My mom's plan was to piece together beloved-turned-bittersweet memories of her boy to create a piece of comfort. When she holds it up to her face, I hope she still smells the muskiness of my brother's cologne and the enthusiasm he brought to our home. The scent of him loving us.

I love the image of God surrounding us with a shield of His favor. And yet, I think it's easy to assume He covers His people with a one-size-fits-all blanket of protection when, really, it's not like that at all. The things God has carefully chosen to surround His people with are His favorite, most beloved pieces of glory. He covers us with an intimacy that sees and knows exactly who we are and what we long for. He gives us compassion that speaks to our booming joys and our secret sorrows. And when we cover ourselves with it at the beginning of the day and settle beneath it at the end, we know we are chosen and loved. Thank the Lord for His favor.

KAITLIN

64

I lift up my eyes to the mountains—
where does my help come from?
My help comes from the LORD,
the Maker of heaven and earth. . . .
The LORD will keep you from all harm—
he will watch over your life.

PSALM 121:1–2, 7

Some call Psalm 121 the soldier's psalm, believing David penned it from the battlefield, trusting God in and between enemy attacks. Others refer to it as the traveler's psalm, written just before a faraway voyage.

Danger calls to us no matter where we are. Therefore, we must also call to God in those same places. While we aren't sure of the psalmist's exact location or intention for this passage, one thing is clear: he has confidence in the Lord. He begins with lifting his eyes up to the hills for help, concluding with assurance in God's watchful eye. No matter what journeys we find ourselves on today, may our comfort begin and end the same way.

KAITLIN

65

Don't be afraid, you who are treasured by
God. Peace to you; be very strong!

DANIEL 10:19 CSB

We are treasured by God. Sometimes we may feel more like a wadded-up tissue on the floor than something worth cherishing. But the wisest Being in the universe looks at you and thinks, *That's My treasure.* Breathe that in for a moment: you are His treasure, and no one can take that away from you.

When we look at ourselves as those who are loved by God, our position in the world feels less vulnerable. The treasure of the Almighty will not go unnoticed. Remember that we are made strong because we are supported by Him. We are His, and we are safe in Him. Don't be afraid, treasured one.

REBECCA

You are Mine

ISAIAH 43:1

66

"I will search for the lost and bring back the strays.
I will bind up the injured and strengthen the weak,
but the sleek and the strong I will destroy.
I will shepherd the flock with justice."

EZEKIEL 34:16

When I read this scripture, I identify with the strays. I wonder if you do too. I have certainly felt weak, lost, and out of place. I have longed for the Lord to bind up my battered heart. And that's exactly what the Lord does and continues to do every day.

This scripture is a comfort to us when we find ourselves weak, unable, and struggling. When we are weak and helpless, the Lord is close by, ready to bring justice and comfort. While we often look at the sleek and the strong, maybe even envying them, this scripture reminds us that God doesn't measure our lives the way the world does. Instead, He shepherds us. He walks with us in our weakness, guides us on good paths that we cannot fathom, and protects us along the way.

Remember the upside-down kingdom Jesus presented to us in the Beatitudes (Matthew 5:3–11)? He gave a laundry list of all the things we'd rather not be and called them blessed: poor, hungry, grieving, and oppressed. And He declared woe on all our favorite things to be: rich, well-fed, happy, and applauded. Jesus was showing us the upside-down kingdom of heaven, where the first are last and the last are first.

If we can turn on our heads for just a second, let our hair brush the floor, and look at the world upside down, we can get a glimpse of what's actually important. Look at who Jesus is looking at. He's looking at the strays. When we find ourselves as strays, we are to run home into His arms, where He binds up our injuries and strengthens our weaknesses.

REBECCA

My cup overflows

67

You prepare a table before me
in the presence of my enemies.
You anoint my head with oil;
my cup overflows.

PSALM 23:5

Growing up, my brother and I were rebellious in the sense that we ate raw cookie dough in secret. While some parents paced until the headlights of their teenagers' borrowed cars shone in the driveway, it must have been the impending threat of raw eggs that kept our mom and dad up at night.

Joined only by each other and the soft glow of the refrigerator bulb, we knew the exact coordinates of the Nestlé Toll House cookie dough—tucked away behind the eggs and just past the cheese. Although the wrapper was closer to the yellow of the school bus we refused to ride together, to us it was gold.

Forming the raw dough into balls as if to pretend their future really did hold a baking sheet, we'd pick out the chocolate chips and eat them first, agreeing that the dough tasted much better that way. It was always a mission with a high risk of getting caught, from a parent suddenly appearing in the hallway during the night to an attempt to make cookies the next day only to discover they've already been eaten.

Comfort found on our own terms always has an expiration date. We know this, and yet, in the middle of the night, we ignore the warnings about raw eggs and self-soothing in the name of sadness or insecurity, pain or boredom. It's enticing and exciting, seemingly harmless at the time. Worse sins have been committed, certainly. And yet, maybe it's not as much about the things we run to in times of desperation as it is about the things we overlook and choose to neglect because we are so self-absorbed.

May our search for comfort not distract us from the table our Good Shepherd has already set for us. He has prepared for us a table, not in secret or in the middle of the night, but in front of our enemies, so that even they may know He is good. With a seat at His table, we are refreshed and find ourselves lacking nothing. We are never alone and are never left to fear (Psalm 23). As His children, we are loved by a Father who knows and responds to our needs. The table has comfort overflowing.

The ramifications of our cookie-dough missions were never something to be proud of. We'd broken the rules, eaten all of the cookies, were up past our bedtimes, and likely crept back upstairs with stomachaches. We'd spoiled something our parents had intended for us to enjoy together as a family. As it turns out, comfort found on our own terms isn't true comfort at all.

But when God catches us in the place of seeking satisfaction on our own and apart from Him, His response is different. His gifts have not run out, and His comfort has not been wasted. He lovingly calls us back to the table, where our seats still wait with abundance overflowing. There's no condemnation—just a better invitation. May we respond with these words: "Surely your goodness and love will follow me all the days of my life, and I will dwell in the house of the LORD forever" (Psalm 23:6).

KAITLIN

68

The LORD gives strength to his people;
the LORD blesses his people with peace.

PSALM 29:11

Living in a converted shuttle bus, two weeks into a summerlong road trip with my husband and five children, I took a pregnancy test in Fargo, North Dakota. Maybe it was the sleep deficit, but when I saw that positive result, I just couldn't stop smiling. Of course God would bless us with another baby at a time when we didn't seem to need one. We certainly didn't have strength and energy left to add morning sickness to every hike and every drive on this long-anticipated trip.

But when it comes to babies, our philosophy is "Have them early and often." When the Lord blesses, we cry, "Yea and amen!" and trust Him to provide the strength for it because we didn't have the strength for any of it. When I look back, I know the Lord has brought us through every surprise and complication with His might because my puny arms never could have done all that heavy lifting.

He gives strength to His own, and He blesses His people with peace. What does that look like? Remember that when Jacob wrestled with an angel at Peniel, the angel injured his hip and told Jacob he'd won. Jacob walked with a limp for the rest of his life from that victory—God's reminder that his strength came only from the Almighty (Genesis 32).

Samson, likewise, believed the strength that God gave him was his own possession. Even after Delilah cut off his hair, Samson still believed that he possessed his strength. But it was never his to begin with. His strength was a gift from God, and when Samson broke his vow, the Lord removed the blessing of strength (Judges 16).

He is our security, our foundation, and our refuge. Paul said, "When I am weak, then I am strong" (2 Corinthians 12:10). Our strength comes from His strength. And the second part of this promise is peace (Psalm 29:11).

God blesses His people with peace. Think of Mary when the angel Gabriel told her she was going to be the mother of the Messiah. Gabriel told her the unimaginable was going to happen, and she responded with "May your word to me be fulfilled" (Luke 1:38). For Mary, peace didn't mean that shocking and scary things didn't come her way; peace meant that when things got complicated God gave her the wisdom to treasure it all up in her heart instead of run screaming back to her parents' house (Luke 1–2).

Paul and Silas found peace even in a prison cell. They sang praises to God even with shackles on their feet. Peace is a stability of mind, not a stability of circumstances. The peace of God keeps our hearts calm in the midst of whatever the world throws at us.

God's people are a motley crew of nighttime wrestlers, long-haired strongmen, scared little girls, and pregnant hikers. We fit right in. God offers us peace and strength the world can't touch—peace that passes all understanding, and strength that's built on an unmoving foundation.

REBECCA

THE Lord BLESSES HIS people WITH PEACE

Ps. 29:11

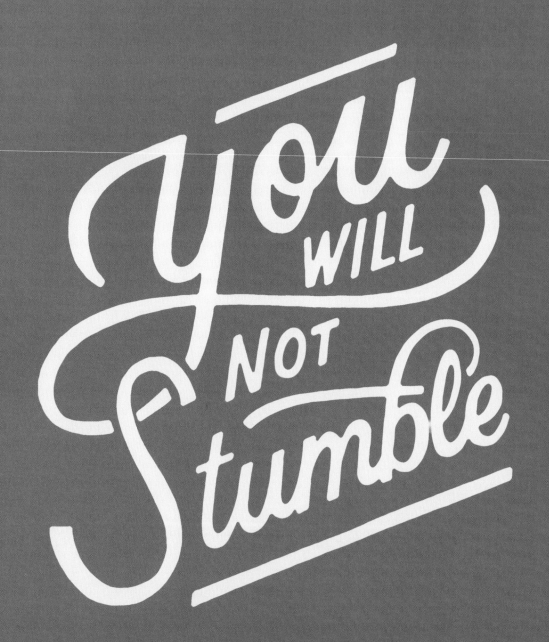

69

When you walk, your steps will not be hampered;
when you run, you will not stumble.

PROVERBS 4:12

So much about the grace and freedom found in the pages of God's Word feels too good to be true. Inside its pages, we find miracles and salvation, grace and the fulfillment we've longed for our whole lives. And at first, when it's all new and gleaming with hope, it's exciting to discover a new way and a deeper reality. We need this life to be better than we thought. But when pain creeps in or the joy begins to dim, it can be difficult to grasp these truths and find comfort in them. Just when we need things to be better and more hopeful than we thought, it's harder to believe it's true.

I love that the cycle of doubt is anticipated and acknowledged in Scripture. When Abraham and Sarah were told they would have a son, Abraham said, "Will a son be born to a man a hundred years old? Will Sarah bear a child at the age of ninety?" (Genesis 17:17). When John heard of Jesus' teachings to His disciples, he asked, "Are you the one who is to come, or should we expect someone else?" (Matthew 11:3).

God knows we're afraid to stumble. He doesn't just set us free to believe whatever sounds best to us at the time—He routinely goes back to the basics because He knows we will forget. He tells us what is true, then reminds us over and over, when we are afraid, lonely, sad, grieving. Even in our fear, it is still true.

KAITLIN

Rest secure
in Him

70

"Let the beloved of the LORD rest secure in him,
for he shields him all day long,
and the one the LORD loves
rests between his shoulders."

DEUTERONOMY 33:12

Children and dogs are such an anomaly on a college campus. As a student, you don't realize you haven't seen anything but students and professors for weeks until something tiny and adorable wanders onto campus, and you are totally undone by the foreign wonder of it. When Caleb and I were in college, two of my elementary-aged siblings came to spend the night with us in the dorms. My sister stayed with me, and my brother stayed with Caleb.

Caleb set up a cozy little bed on the floor for Jordan, but my brother was just a little guy, so during the night he found his way to the top bunk, to snuggle with someone warm, and nestled right between Caleb's shoulders. The next morning we were struck by this little sweet and safe gesture.

The Lord shields us all day long, and we are safe to rest between His shoulders. It's an image of tender love and safety. We are the beloved of the Lord, and He invites us to nestle in His security and warm loving-kindness.

REBECCA

THE LORD HAS
Compassion

71

As a father has compassion on his children,
so the LORD has compassion on those who fear him.

PSALM 103:13

I have been blessed with a godly father, with wonderful grandfathers, and with other godly mentors. In times of doubt and in times of struggle, there is nothing like the comfort of a father who knows, who loves, and who encourages. In a recent season of grief, my pastor, who has been a father figure for me in many ways, said, "This will be hard, but I will walk with you through it. God's grace is sufficient for even this."

How does a father comfort? He knows the needs of his children. He knows the weakness of their frames. He knows their frailty and their sorrows. He knows. But more than this, he walks with them. And our heavenly Father walks with us. He does not promise that there will be no difficulty, but that He will have compassion on us and remain with us through the darkest and most difficult trials. He knows how we are formed and remembers that we are dust.

In weakness, cry out, "Abba! Father!" He is your strength. In your wandering, His are the hands that reach out to restore. In your sorrow and pain, His are the arms that lift you up. He is full of compassion and abounding in mercy.

CALEB

Comfort in Truth

The king will rejoice in God;
all who swear by God will glory in him,
while the mouths of liars will be silenced.

PSALM 63:11

God doesn't give easy answers to difficult questions. His timing, His purpose, His promise of fulfillment are not bound by our human, earthly, and fleshly understanding. His truth is eternal. The comfort He offers is eternal. Our pining for comfort here, where the grass withers and the flower fades, is ultimately answered by God's Word, which endures forever.

CALEB

72

Those who hope in the LORD
will renew their strength.
They will soar on wings like eagles;
they will run and not grow weary,
they will walk and not be faint.

ISAIAH 40:31

Matthew Henry, in his *Concise Commentary on the Whole Bible*, said, "If we go forth in our own strength, we shall faint, and utterly fall; but having our hearts and our hopes in heaven, we shall be carried above all difficulties, and be enabled to lay hold of the prize of our high calling in Christ Jesus."

It is when our own strength is depleted that we are more than ever able to soar, run, walk, and hope. If our end goal is eternal life with our Father, pain is no longer a stumbling block, but an open gate. Here we are, together—every ache leading us closer to hope. May our strength be marked not by our stamina, but by our closeness to Christ.

KAITLIN

YOU WILL SEE *Greater* THINGS — THAN THAT

73

*"You believe because I told you I saw you under the
fig tree. You will see greater things than that."*

J O H N   1 : 5 0

Do you believe that Jesus is the Christ?

Nathanael, sitting beneath the fig tree, was slow to believe. His trustworthy friend Philip brought him news of the Messiah, urging him earnestly to come and see the Christ. But not until Nathanael heard Jesus' miraculous insight—that Jesus had seen him under the tree before Philip even arrived—did he believe.

Since that time, we have had the witness of more than two thousand years. Christ performed miracles greater than the one Nathanael experienced that day. He made the lame to walk, the blind to see, the lepers to be clean, the dead to be alive again. Jesus is the Christ, and He has come. He walked the soil of this earth, bled, died, was buried beneath this ground, and rose again.

To all who looked to Him for answers to their prayers, He said, "I am willing. . . . Be clean. . . . Rise up and walk" (Mark 1:41; Luke 5:23 KJV).

To all who looked to Him for salvation, He said, "Your sins are forgiven" (Matthew 9:2).

Yet to Nathanael, He made this promise: "You will see 'heaven open, and the angels of God ascending and descending on' the Son of Man" (John 1:51).

Jesus Himself is the answer to our every prayer. He is the resurrection and the life. He is the ascended One. He is the Christ.

We often find ourselves, like Nathanael, waiting beneath the fig tree, praying for God's answers. We pray for healing, for guidance, for joy, for hope, for provision, for newness of life. There we wait, wondering when we will see His promise fulfilled, His promise to wipe away every tear (Revelation 7:17), to remove all mourning, crying, and pain (Revelation 21:4).

When our eyes grow dim, and we lose sight of the eternal vision, we forget these greater things that are to come, the glories that lie ahead. We sit beneath our fig trees, waiting, wondering if God sees us. We find the answers in front of us dissatisfying, incomplete, and confusing. And that is always the way of the here and now. As hard as they are, these sorrows are also for our good because they drive us to pray beneath the fig tree, and they motivate us to get up and look for answers. "Lord, I believe; help my unbelief!" (Mark 9:24 NKJV).

When we hear the voice that says, "Come and see" (John 1:39 NKJV), it is the voice calling us to our true Comfort, to the one and only answer to all our prayers. We were not made to be satisfied by the things of this earth. These things will all pass away (Matthew 24:35).

We were made for the glory that awaits. We were made for eternity. We were made for Christ, who sees us where we are, who knows us, who wipes away every tear, who makes all things new, who has prepared greater things than we have seen.

God sees you where you are. He sees you and He knows you. Christ beckons. Come and see.

CALEB

74

And the peace of God, which transcends all understanding,
will guard your hearts and your minds in Christ Jesus.

PHILIPPIANS 4:7

There are many days when I just want to turn my phone off and make the texts stop coming. Too many calls and emails overwhelm my brain, and I can't get a moment of stillness to focus. Often I'm interrupted by the playing and fighting of my children too.

The people nudging me with all these notifications are mostly beloved friends, and while we're in this busy season of life, I have to give ear to a lot of these voices. However, if we can't make all the noise stop, how can we ever find peace? And if my peace is dependent on my control of my circumstances, will I ever have enough control to achieve peace? Is it possible to have peace in the midst of all this laughing, playing, fighting, and buzzing?

As a celibate first-century man, Paul wasn't rattled by buzzing notifications and noisy kids. Regardless of what is jarring you, Paul was talking about peace that transcends all understanding. Peace in the thick of it. Peace on the battlefield. Peace in the trenches. It's easy for me to understand peace at the ocean or peace on the massage table. But the peace that passes understanding is peace in spite of any circumstances.

This is the mighty peace of God that will guard our hearts and minds. His peace will guard us from losing our minds in the jangly, everyday hubbub, and His peace is powerful enough to guard our hearts even in seemingly unbearable suffering.

Jesus paid for our peace with His life: "He was pierced because of our rebellion, crushed because of our iniquities; punishment for our peace was on him, and we are healed by his wounds" (Isaiah 53:5 CSB). The punishment for our peace was on Him! What an astonishing truth! Because of His sacrifice, we win the hard-fought gem of peace that passes all understanding. Thanks be to God.

REBECCA

AND THE PEACE OF GOD WHICH
TRANSCENDS ALL UNDERSTANDING

WILL GUARD YOUR HEARTS
AND MINDS IN CHRIST JESUS

75

*"Can a mother forget the baby at her breast
and have no compassion on the child she has borne?
Though she may forget,
I will not forget you!"*

ISAIAH 49:15

Memories grow fuzzy, and belongings go missing; neighbors move away, and our feelings move on. All of these forgotten items have one thing in common: they have been left. But the Lord our God won't forget us because He will never abandon us.

I recently held a sleeping newborn baby at a party, giving his mother the opportunity to fill her plate with food and mingle with other guests. But the entire time her watchful and compassionate gaze did not leave her son. She could hear a single squirm from across the room, knowing immediately he was waking up and would be hungry.

God's gaze never leaves us either. There is no instance where we are past tense to Him; never will we catch Him on an off day when He neglects to love us. He remembers and cherishes us, even now.

KAITLIN

FOR THE LORD LOVES THE JUST AND WILL NOT FORSAKE HIS FAITHFUL ONES.

76

For the LORD loves the just
and will not forsake his faithful ones.
Wrongdoers will be completely destroyed;
the offspring of the wicked will perish.

PSALM 37:28

Judgment is the hot potato of faith: sinners are afraid to hold it. Our experience with God's wrath is so limited that we readily choose the warmth of His character rather than the fire of His wrath, never lingering long enough to learn they are of the same flame.

God's wrath is not anger for the sake of anger or an excuse to exercise His power. Rather, it is His reaction to something that hurts the people He loves. Sin makes God angry because He intimately knows the ways it hurts us and separates us from Him. At the root of God's wrath is a desire to set things right.

Let us trust in our Father, who doesn't judge out of obligation and power, but out of a desire to protect His people and delight in them. He loves justice because He loves us.

KAITLIN

77

My times are in your hands;
deliver me from the hands of my enemies,
from those who pursue me.

PSALM 31:15

The phrase "My times are in your hands" is just wonderful, isn't it? It conjures up an idea of safety and purpose that whisks away all my small thoughts about multitasking and time management. But what does it mean? Some translators render this as "My future is in your hands" (CEB; GW). Although it's less surprising, I like that too. Another translation says, "The course of my life is in your power" (CSB), which is wonderfully evocative of a seafaring life with Christ as the captain. And the good old King James Version agrees with the NIV and translates this as "My times are in thy hand."

The word most often translated as "time" comes from the Hebrew word עֵת, which is found elsewhere in the Bible as "times," "experiences," and "fortunes." It is used to refer to specific times of life, and even specific times of day. It is used in significant moments, such as "the time has come," and for whole seasons.

What the psalmist was trying to say here is our evenings and our mornings are in God's care. Our birthdays and our funerals are in His hands. Our winters and our springtimes are under His power. Our wedding days and our Tuesday nights are sheltered and guided by One who does not sleep or slumber, One who loves us with an everlasting love.

REBECCA

78

You will surely forget your trouble,
recalling it only as waters gone by.

JOB 11:16

Most of my childhood took place on a pontoon boat. Growing up in a house surrounded by banana trees and lake water seemed to be our family's reward for enduring hot and humid Florida summers and faithfully keeping the sunscreen industry afloat.

As soon as my dad would come home from work, he'd put on a baseball cap and head to the backyard. Then we'd run barefoot through the grass and sit next to him on the dock, our feet dangling in the air above a flock of ducks that gathered each night. They anxiously waited for the bread crumbs stowed away in our pockets. We would feed the birds as my dad untied the knots docking the boat.

All the while, the water remained still, only moving with the swim patterns of the duck family or from the wake of a neighbor's canoe. It was sure and safe, usually allowing us to pile into the boat with blankets and snacks, just in time for sunset.

That's the thing about lakes: the water only moves when it's told. While it was always dependably waiting for us in the same place for our next after-school adventure, the downside was that any fallen branches or debris from harsh thunderstorms would stick around patiently too.

Sometimes I assume that my pain and trouble, both past and present, will never move along. Or if it does, the responsibility for moving it will all be up to me. But God's Word tells us something

You will surely forget your trouble,
recalling it only as waters gone by

different: "You will surely forget your trouble, recalling it only as waters gone by."

This encouragement was given to Job after he had faced some of history's most deeply documented pain—physical, emotional, and spiritual. Job's friend assured him that even one of the most hopeless moments would eventually be forgotten and redeemed by God's hand.

The waters of our suffering do not pool into a still-watered lake. Rather, they have the fluidity of a stream, moving with the ebb of eternity and flow of God's grace. They don't respond to our unsure movements, but to the commands of our Father, whose will is perfect and whose character is sure.

KAITLIN

HE
WILL NOT
ABANDON

79

The LORD your God is a merciful God; he will not
abandon or destroy you or forget the covenant with your
ancestors, which he confirmed to them by oath.

DEUTERONOMY 4:31

One of my earliest memories is the parking lot at the church my parents helped plant in Taipei. I remember it because one Sunday, in a moment of enthusiasm, I ran ahead of my parents to beat them to the car. When I arrived at the blue sedan, it was not our car, and my parents were not in sight. The parking lot suddenly looked a lot bigger and stranger. I can still picture row upon row of cars, and the blue one that was not ours, and no one in sight, and the tall buildings of Taiwan surrounding me. I did not even know which direction to call out.

When we wander, we find ourselves in strange and terrifying places. We can wander in any number of ways: in our affections, our goals, our desires, our priorities, our focus, even our trust. We forget which way we have come from, which way we were going. But God does not forget. He remembers His promises to be faithful even when we doubt, even when we are faithless. He will not abandon His children.

I remember seeing my mom round the corner of the faraway row and the way she ran toward me, arms open, ready to scoop me up. God never loses track of us. He knows even our wanderings. And He is ready and able to bring us back. When we do not know the way home, He is still there. He Himself is the way home. He is the faithful One who does not forget. He is the Rescuer, mighty to save. Look for Him. Seek Him with all your heart and with all your soul. Return to Him, for He loves you with an everlasting love.

CALEB

80

*"Whoever touches you touches
the apple of his eye."*

ZECHARIAH 2:8

I learned to sew in my late twenties. My mother-in-law gave me a sewing machine as an engagement gift, but nothing could persuade me to use it until we had a baby girl, and I realized it could be used to produce tiny, flouncy dresses. When Beatrice was three, she was the perfect size for dresses made from just one yard of fabric, and I lost no time figuring a basic theme for dresses and then hurried to create variations on that theme. For hours, she and I would sit in a quiet room, smelling the sharp steam from the iron and hearing the whirr of the sewing machine. She lifted heavy green pattern weights to drape fabric from her tiny ironing board to the windowsill and made up long, quiet songs about girls and dresses.

The garments I made during that year are woefully imperfect. I used ribbons where I should have sewn straps, I left waistbands unfinished where I should have done French seams, and there were hemlines that just dragged on the floor with strings trailing behind. But those little dresses comprise the most beautiful designer collection my eyes have ever seen.

It's possible that I have an unreasonable attachment to those dresses because I made them with my own hands with my tiniest darling at my side. I know there are things and people for whom you harbor wonderful, doesn't-work-on-paper adoration. I acknowledge that it's possible my husband isn't the handsomest, wisest man on the planet, but I only have eyes for him.

God made us, and we are the apple of His eye. Who can march around us and judge our worth when the King of kings has declared us His own? No one can weigh and measure our accomplishments because no one's scale matters but His. God's people are loved with an everlasting loving-kindness that isn't based on how we fail or succeed. He has called us by His own name, and we are His.

Our worth begins and ends with the Lord. This lifts so much tension for me. It cuts out the urgency of the rat race and keeping up with the neighbors. Instead, we can look to Him and His Word for our measuring stick. And time after time, the Lord shows that He is merciful and loving to His people—beyond what we could ever earn.

And when we measure our strengths and weaknesses against His ruler, we can see that at our worst moments we fall embarrassingly short, but even at our best moments we are still missing His mark of perfection. Even our righteousness is as filthy rags (Isaiah 64:6).

But He forgives our sins and our attempts at righteousness and sees Christ's snow-white garments instead. He looks at us with eyes of love. He is inexplicably attached to us. He loves us in spite of our slipping hemlines and our mismatched seams. We are His children, and we are the apple of His eye.

REBECCA

81

This is what the LORD says to Israel: "Seek me and live."

AMOS 5:4

I imagine your to-do list is long today. It seems as if I never quite come to the end of mine, no matter how efficiently I conduct my day. And I know that if you're suffering, a completely ordinary list can swell to completely unmanageable proportions. The prospect of a simple phone call can easily fill one with dread for a whole day. But look at this pithy and delightful to-do list from Amos: seek God and live.

Doesn't it make you sigh with relief? The first thing on the list is "Seek God." Start there. Wake up each morning with your compass pointing toward Him. Set your feet in His direction. Let the pursuit of God be your first priority . . . and then live.

REBECCA

HOW ABUNDANT ARE THE GOOD THINGS

82

How abundant are the good things
that you have stored up for those who fear you,
that you bestow in the sight of all,
on those who take refuge in you.

PSALM 31:19

What are these abundant good things David was talking about in today's scripture? We certainly love the idea of an abundance of good things stored up for us. And in dry times, I like to think about what goodness the Lord has for me now and has stored up for later. Just from Psalm 31, here are some good things that David believed God will be for His people:

- a protector from shame (v. 1)
- a listening ear (v. 2)
- a strong fortress (v. 2)
- a guide (v. 3)
- a source of unfailing love (v. 16)
- a shelter (v. 20)
- our safety (v. 20)
- our source of mercy (v. 22)

Don't look for your refuge in things that won't last when all this richness is already promised to you. Stand secure today in the hope we share for the abundant good things God has for those who take refuge in Him.

REBECCA

83

He who was seated on the throne said, "I am making
everything new!" Then he said, "Write this down,
for these words are trustworthy and true."

REVELATION 21:5

There are some pains that endure our whole lives long, some aches that never fully go away. Some losses will never fully heal, and some longings will never be fulfilled. But this life is only the briefest part of our story.

Christ is seated on the throne, and He is making all things new. *All things*. He cares about our loves and losses, and He will set things right for all of eternity.

Although we may grieve for this short season, Christ beckons us with eternity—where our sorrows are washed away, our losses are returned, and our longings are fulfilled in Him. Set your hope on Him who is making all things new.

REBECCA

I WILL GIVE YOU REST

84

*"Come to me, all you who are weary and
burdened, and I will give you rest."*

MATTHEW 11:28

I learned to play the piano when I was seven. After years of watching my mother and grandmother command their hands and feet to play keys and push pedals to create a familiar melody that rattled the wood floors, my own lessons were a long-awaited rite of passage.

One afternoon a week, my teacher, Mrs. Griffin, would ring the doorbell of our family home, holding a stack of songbooks under one arm. She'd scoot our old leather bench from under the piano and position herself next to me. Then she would open the beginner book and teach me all about the black and white lines and spaces on the page, how the positioning of each symbol meant a different note, a separate key, a changing rhythm. She'd clap the cadence of each line, showing how some notes were meant to be played faster, others held longer, and some not played at all. I began to doubt that the music on the page could communicate the fullness of the sounds I'd grown up hearing. Certainly, my mother and grandmother had learned another way.

But then one day I learned the true difference between notes and rests. I'd known that the funny little symbol at the end of the line meant to stop pressing down the keys immediately, but what I didn't realize was their importance in the work of art. Sound and silence were equally part of each song, neither more important than the other and both holding the power to hurt the other. Too much sound and not enough silence would cause the sound to chaotically rush together, and too much silence would prevent the listener from hearing the song's intended wholeness.

When I was no longer playing the music by ear, creating my own pace and rhythms, I realized the purpose of the sheet music. For the first time, I was careful to hold rests for their full counts, and surprisingly, it was the first time the wooden floors rattled in that old familiar way. The key to a full sound was observing the rest before and after it.

I'm just as guilty of playing physical rest by ear, going at my own pace and rhythm. And yet, God has already written the tune and established the tempo for us. He calls us to hold a long rest day of Sabbath, a place to catch and take in our breath between weeks. But Sabbath isn't just a day to drop everything only to pick it back up the next day. It's a day that sets rest as the rhythm and tone of our lives.

In some seasons, God may give us rest more deeply and fully, and in others, we may feel as though we're gasping for air, unable to catch a break. Yet this is exactly how He wants us to come to Him—weary and burdened. He will give us rest.

May we lean into our pain and our joys, listening closely to the underlying call to rest in Christ's withness. May it be a full and glorious sound of praise.

KAITLIN

85

*No one who hopes in you
will ever be put to shame.*

PSALM 25:3

My friend Katie loves jet streams. She'd want me to make it clear that the technical name for the line-shaped clouds that follow airplanes is *contrail*, but for her purposes and now ours, they are known simply as jet streams.

Ask her why she loves them so much and you'll soon recognize this is Katie's favorite question to answer. Giddy and unable to sit still, she'll lean in to tell you the story as if it's her best-kept secret. She'll recall the first time she stood in a place where she felt very stuck, and a jet stream in the sky made her feel as though God saw her situation and promised to give her a way out. And even now, years later, jet streams remind Katie of the ways God has kept His promises in the past and of the hope that He will continue to do so again and again.

After God granted victory to Israel over her enemies in the promised land, Samuel raised a large stone in remembrance of what God had done for His people and named it Ebenezer (1 Samuel 7:12). Much later, hymn writer Robert Robinson would reference this stone in a verse of "Come, Thou Fount of Every Blessing." It reads, "Here I raise my Ebenezer." We all need a reminder to keep going with our belief that faith is worth the long haul.

Hope bridges our humanity to God's holiness. It is what tells us that things are going to be okay even as they are falling apart. It is what allows us to see our pain without drowning in the depths of it. It is what reminds us that Someone else is fighting on our behalf and that we don't have to go at it alone.

Even now, years after the first jet stream encounter, Katie will stop mid-sentence or pull over on the side of the road to take in streaks in the sky. And even now, they remind her of the ways God has been and will continue to be good and faithful to her, in ways she didn't and still can't begin to see.

The hope He gives to us is more than optimism or compassion. It's steady and true. Whether it's through tangible reminders of God's presence or the promises He made to us in His Word, His faithfulness is strong enough to carry us. It hasn't failed us before, and it will not fail us today.

May we watch in anticipation for the ways hope is shouting our names today.

KAITLIN

86

The LORD will guide you always;
he will satisfy your needs in a sun-scorched land
and will strengthen your frame.
You will be like a well-watered garden,
like a spring whose waters never fail.

ISAIAH 58:11

I had only seen the desert in pictures, and I grew up in the Midwest, so the whole landscape of my life was green and leafy. Shade is a given in Michigan. As we bumped over the hills of South Dakota for the first time on a road trip out west, we delighted over the fuzzy, yellow grass on the foreign landscape. But when we finally spotted the Badlands in the distance, my jaw dropped at the rough red-and-white-striped hills.

This land was alien and scorched by the sun. There wasn't a tree in sight, and the sun had baked the hills into crumbly, dry, dusty clay. Nothing could grow, and almost nothing could live there. Just a few hours out in the sun drove us to Wall Drug for air-conditioning and relief. Later that night, when we settled down to camp, even though the sun had already set, the ground was radiating heat.

There are seasons when our hearts are like that parched land. We feel shriveled up and out of life. We can't escape from these seasons with a quick trip to Wall Drug (or with TV, or vacation, or food, or relationships, or whatever we use to find release); the sweet relief we long for comes from Christ. He offers refreshment to those who follow Him.

First, to find His relief, we are called to trust in His guidance, which we find in Scripture. As we learn to love what He loves and seek it, we will naturally experience relief because of our simple and beautiful alignment with Christ.

Second, to enjoy this relief, we are called to look to Him for satisfaction. All the things that beckon us will ultimately disappoint because Christ is the only true satisfaction. The natural consequence of looking to Christ is the relief from the sure disappointment of any other source.

In the light of His guidance and His satisfaction, we are no longer a sun-scorched people, but we are like well-watered gardens—full of lush life and overflowing with blessings to share. Jesus reaches out to us in our desert days and offers Himself, the Living Water, to bring the relief we are longing for.

REBECCA

THE LORD
WILL GUIDE YOU
ALWAYS

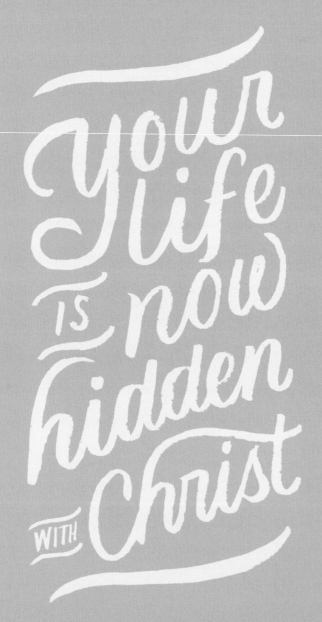

87

You died, and your life is now hidden with Christ in God.

COLOSSIANS 3:3

Christ takes the worst possible news and turns it into the best. Our death is not naturally considered a grace or grounds on which to find hope, but because of God's love for us, it is. Because of the way He looks at us, our lives are neither too much nor not enough to be hidden with Him in His glory. The things we've done that bring us shame and the things done to us that bring us pain—all died with Christ and have been replaced with His clean record.

He hides us as a means of protection and separation from the things that hurt us. He hides us to set our hearts and minds on eternal joy. He hides us to move us closer to Him and His kingdom. He hides us because He loves us and is bringing us back to life.

KAITLIN

88

Today I am freeing you from the chains on your wrists.

JEREMIAH 40:4

My favorite word in this verse is easy to skip over: *today.* And yet, it was a word that meant everything to those held in captivity in Babylon. After they were taken away, it seemed as if their story was over because their circumstances were looking bleak. Without much hope of escape, they probably thought similarly.

But their story wasn't over. The long-awaited day of freedom came. The prophecies came true. God's promises remained. The doubting was over.

Because of Christ's resurrection, we truly have freedom *today.* Our hope is sealed. Today we find comfort in our Father. Today He is faithful to us.

KAITLIN

I am freeing you

I AM THE FIRST

AND THE LAST

89

When I saw him, I fell at his feet as though dead. Then he placed his right hand on me and said: "Do not be afraid. I am the First and the Last. I am the Living One; I was dead, and now look, I am alive for ever and ever! And I hold the keys of death and Hades."

REVELATION 1:17–18

Our eyes have not seen and our minds cannot comprehend the glory that awaits us in Christ. When one day we behold Him as He is, the worries and fears, the sorrows and troubles of this present life will grow strangely dim. The things in this life that have undone us will themselves be undone.

Have you been overwhelmed as John was in today's scripture? Have you found yourself shaken by your cares, by your sorrows, by your fears? Then fall at the feet of Christ. He desires that you be overcome by His grace. When we are undone at His feet, He bends low to reach for us. He stoops to conquer for all who are His. His hand of comfort, of healing, of peace, of love, He extends. His face, which shines as the brightest sun, He turns toward us in love and favor.

What, then, shall we fear if the Son of the living God has granted us His peace and comfort? It is true that this life is full of troubles. The trials we face may seem to have no answer and perhaps may seem to have no ending. Yet they will end, and they will be answered. They have been answered already in Christ's priceless blood, shed for His children. They are being answered even now as Christ our advocate intercedes for us at the throne of grace. They will be answered in full when we see Him in glory.

He holds the keys of death and Hades. It is not the Devil that rules death and hell. It is not the world that rules our lives and our fates. Christ is Lord of all. In this world we will have troubles, but He has overcome the world (John 16:33), death, and the evil one, and He holds the keys of death and Hades. If we are His, what have we to fear?

CALEB

CONCLUSION

*The LORD will watch over your coming and going
both now and forevermore.*

P S A L M 1 2 1 : 8

We opened this book by talking about God alone as our source of provision. Then we explored praise as a response to God's actions in our lives. After that we got in the trenches with darkness and honestly looked at both why we need comfort and how God meets our darkness with light. We looked at hope and restoration and how Jesus brings justice to things that look as though they will never be set right. And in the last section we offered the hope that all wrongs will be righted in eternity. There might not be earthly solutions to our suffering, but ultimately, eternity sets everything in perspective. Dancing and feasting and joy will have the final say at the feet of Christ in heaven.

The last words we leave you are the words of Psalm 121. If you are hurting, look to the true source of your help. He will protect you during the day and the night; He will watch out for you in ways you don't even know to watch out for yourself. He looks at you with eyes of love, both now and forevermore.

> I lift up my eyes to the mountains—
> where does my help come from?
> My help comes from the LORD,

the Maker of heaven and earth.
He will not let your foot slip—
he who watches over you will not slumber;
indeed, he who watches over Israel
will neither slumber nor sleep.
The LORD watches over you—
the LORD is your shade at your right hand;
the sun will not harm you by day,
nor the moon by night.
The LORD will keep you from all harm—
he will watch over your life;
the LORD will watch over your coming and going
both now and forevermore.

CALEB FAIRES was trained in drawing since childhood, and he just can't shake those early lessons. He has spent his life drawing and studied illustration, painting, and sculpture at Hillsdale College in Michigan. He has been fortunate to illustrate and design for private collectors, ad campaigns, and publishers. He also serves as a professor at New College Franklin, teaching drawing and sculpture. In addition to his artwork, Caleb is a contributing writer at He Reads Truth. He lives in a log cabin in Tennessee with his lovely wife and five children, where he continues to illustrate and write.

REBECCA FAIRES loves the gospel story. And she needs it every morning when she wakes up to raise her five little people. Rebecca holds a bachelor's degree from Hillsdale College in German, and most recently worked as the managing editor and writer at She Reads Truth. She now works from home to live her dream of writing and illustrating books with her favorite mountain man. They work from a log cabin in the hills of Tennessee, where she enjoys sitting on the porch when it rains, surprises gone terribly wrong, baby hummingbirds, the Oxford English Dictionary, and getting in way over her head.

KAITLIN WERNET is a storyteller surrendered to hope. Forever passionate about holding the tension of darkness and light, she is grateful for the Good News that acknowledges and redeems both. With a journalism degree from the University of South Carolina, she spends her days writing everything from marketing strategies and prizeworthy puns to nonfiction essays and She Reads Truth devotionals. Living in Nashville, Tennessee, by way of Asheville, North Carolina, she's always planning her next big travel adventure but vows to only plant roots in cities that rhyme.

CYMONE WILDER is a Nashville based designer, lettering artist, and sometimes photographer. She holds a degree in Art from Olivet Nazarene University, and has a professional, marketing-focused design background. She is fiercely passionate about producing meaningful and long-lasting work, drawing inspiration from the very real and analog world around her. Since 2013 she has collaborated with amazing clients—creating custom lettering artwork for established brands, bibles, books, apparel, and much more.